THEATRE SYMPOSIUM
A PUBLICATION OF THE SOUTHEASTERN THEATRE CONFERENCE

Ritual, Religion, and Theatre

Volume 21

D1710059

Published by the

Southeastern Theatre Conference and

The University of Alabama Press

THEATRE SYMPOSIUM is published annually by the Southeastern Theatre Conference, Inc. (SETC), and by The University of Alabama Press. SETC nonstudent members receive the journal as a part of their membership under rules determined by SETC. For information on membership write to SETC, P.O. Box 9868, Greensboro, NC 27429-0868. All other inquiries regarding subscriptions, circulation, purchase of individual copies, and requests to reprint materials should be addressed to The University of Alabama Press, Box 870380, Tuscaloosa, AL 35487-0380.

THEATRE SYMPOSIUM publishes works of scholarship resulting from a single-topic meeting held on a southeastern university campus each spring. A call for papers to be presented at that meeting is widely publicized each autumn for the following spring. Authors are encouraged to send unsolicited manuscripts directly to the editor. Information about the next symposium is available from the incoming editor, David S. Thompson, Department of Theatre, Agnes Scott College, 141 E. College Avenue, Decatur, GA, 30030, dthompson@agnesscott.edu.

THEATRE SYMPOSIUM
A PUBLICATION OF THE SOUTHEASTERN THEATRE CONFERENCE

Volume 21   *Contents*   **2013**

Introduction

E. Bert Wallace

THE TITLE of this volume is a bit of a compromise. Many, some with good reason, are rather repulsed by the word "religion." Visions of hidden agendas, of proselytizers and fundamentalists of various stripes, loom. "Spirituality" was briefly considered and quickly discarded. In the end, in lieu of another word, "ritual" was added to broaden the call. Whether or not theatre arose from ritual or religion or both, from prehistory to the present there have been clear and vital connections among the three.

My own comingling of religion and theatre has been both vocational and avocational. Because I majored in theatre in college, I was often called upon to "put a little skit together" for various church occasions as a student and into my adulthood. For many years, I've been associated with Christians in Theatre Arts (CITA), an organization that has greatly encouraged my scholarship, theatrical practice, and faith. And I'm currently the chair of the Religion and Theatre Committee for SETC and the head of the Drama & Christian Ministry Program at Campbell University, where I continue to write and direct plays in which religion, or ritual, or faith is enacted on the stage. The topic for my second volume as editor of *Theatre Symposium* flowed naturally from my own scholarship and creative work.

I was delighted that Dr. Tom F. Driver agreed to serve as our keynote speaker and conference respondent. His lifetime of work exactly coincides with our threefold focus. His address on the opening night of the conference is printed in this volume. We all sat enthralled; several attendees told me that his was the best keynote address they'd ever heard. Dr. Driver graciously attended all the sessions and held a conference response and discussion at the end of the event.

As I hoped, our topic drew a wide variety of scholars. Of course, not every paper can be published (for a variety of reasons), but the presented papers not published here deserve some mention. Bradley Stephenson (University of Missouri–Columbia) drew on his experiences as a fraternity pledge to discuss initiation rituals; Chris Peck (Baylor University) presented a case study about a conservative audience response to a controversial play; Joan Lazarus (University of Texas–Austin) spoke on religion and spirituality in secondary theatre education; Eric Kildow (Coastal Carolina Community College) drew parallels between Puritan and Platonic antitheatrical prejudice; Karen Polit (University of Heidelberg) spoke on her fieldwork with tribal ritual in the Himalayas; Amanda Sweeney (University of Chicago) explored how religion dramatizes the divine; and Erin Hopkins (New York University) and Brenna Nicely (University of Central Florida) presented separately on historical Christmas pageants.

Several presenters at this year's conference included performance as part of their presentation. In particular, Greg Carr (whose paper is printed here) enacted the call-and-response and "whoops" of the traditional black preacher that his paper discussed, greatly enhancing the audience's understanding. Another honored guest, Association for Theatre in Higher Education (ATHE) president Dr. William Doan, performed as well; excerpts of Bill's performances are printed at the end of this volume.

I must give special thanks to Andy Belser of the University of North Carolina–Wilmington, our host school. Andy was immensely helpful from the moment I approached him about having the conference at Wilmington. Thanks also go to former editors Phil Hill, J. K. Curry, and Scott Phillips for all their help and support; former editor Paul Castagno of UNC-W, who was my graduate advisor at the University of Alabama and very supportive of this conference; Betsey Baun, Quiana Clark-Roland, and all the staff at the SETC central office for their support; Dan Waterman, Debbie Upton, Crissie Johnson, and the staff of the University of Alabama Press; Trey Morehouse, our tireless student worker who drove us all over Wilmington; Becky Jurius, my student assistant at Campbell University; Ran Whitley, Georgia Martin, and all my supportive colleagues at Campbell; and, most importantly, Kelley, Peter, and Betsy Wallace. My family has been almost unbelievably supportive of all the effort it has taken to organize two conferences and get two volumes to press. My thanks—and all my love—go to them.

Keynote Address

"The Blessed Assurance of Perhaps"

Tom F. Driver

I N THE INTERVIEW that I was fortunate to have with him, Samuel
Beckett said, "The key word in my plays is 'perhaps.'" You have to
love a playwright who will say things like that.

When my granddaughter was of preschool age, she loved to play with
the subjunctive mood. We had a game in which I would make up a sentence including the word "maybe." She would answer, "And maybe not!"
The child, like the playwright, enjoyed playing outside, though not too
far outside, the boundary of things necessarily so. In other words, they
both delighted in the exercise of imagination. Yet they wanted their what-
ifs to hover not far from what is. And so do I.

Unlike the movies, theatre is not a dream factory but a playground.
The fun of a playground is that you are really in it, not dreaming that you
are in it. You might really fall off the jungle gym and hurt yourself. You
really do chute down through gravity on the sliding board. And yet you
are at play. Not in the sense of pretending—not, if you will, playacting—
but playing *with*.

When I was an undergraduate at Duke University, a man named Bill
Poteat taught philosophy there. Arriving home one afternoon, he found
his small daughter and some friends her age in the living room, all absorbed in a game on the floor. Bill asked what they were playing and was
told a name he'd never heard before. Invited to play with them, he sat
down and asked, "What are the rules of the game?" His daughter indig-
nantly replied: "The only rule is that you can't cheat!"

So there, in case you were wondering, is my aesthetic: freedom combined with total honesty. "Maybe not" looking back over its shoulder at
"maybe." Not just anything that *could* be, but something that *might* be.
The key word is "perhaps."

Beckett also commented on the religion of his homeland. He said to me, "Ireland is *so* religious. You expect to wake up one morning and see all the dogs crossing themselves."

We may not be in Ireland, but we are in the Bible Belt, perhaps the most religious part of a quirkily religious nation. Beckett's quip about the dogs of Ireland cuts close to home—except that here the dogs would bark, "Praise the Lord!"

I was born in the Bible Belt, in eastern Tennessee. From the time of my earliest memories I was enamored of both religion and theatre. It did not occur to me that there was any conflict between them until my father told me that when he was a student at Ohio Wesleyan University— just before World War I—a classmate of his had been expelled from the school because he had gone to see something in a theatre. Not to a bur- lesque house or a vaudeville show, mind you, but to a play by William Shakespeare. By the time my father told me this some twenty-five years after the fact, Ohio Wesleyan was boasting a strong theatre program of its own.

The nineteenth-century Danish philosopher and theologian Søren Kierkegaard spent some time as a young man writing theatre criticism for a newspaper in Berlin. He later complained that people went to the theatre looking for what they ought to find in church, and they went to church looking for what they ought to find in the theatre. But the worst of it, he said, was that they actually found it!

That lament seems to come from the same point of view as that of T. S. Eliot when he said that liturgy *seems* like drama but in truth is *not* drama. To which I say, "Perhaps."

There cannot be a productive relation between religion and theatre when religion is identified with its dogma. The dogmatist abhors perhap- sness. From my perspective, however, dogmatism stifles not only theatre but also true religion, because it stifles the imagination.

In his book *The Religious Case against Belief*, James Carse suggests that religions, which are the longest-surviving institutions in the world, endure because they generate endless conversation.[1] As Beckett's Didi might say, it is not enough for religions to exist—they have to talk about it.[2] This would not be so if religious teachings admitted of certainty. But of course they do not.

Biblical Job may say, "I know that my redeemer liveth," and Handel may set us to singing those words with a mighty chorus, but the book of Job itself is a long argument with and about God. However strong Job's conviction or faith, it does not answer his questions. It is not enough for him to live and to suffer. He has to talk about it—because he cannot be certain.

So that's the first point I've wanted to make today: something I might call the blessed assurance of "perhaps."

When Bert Wallace called to invite me to the 2012 Theatre Symposium, he made the invitation irresistible by saying the conference theme would be "ritual, religion, and theatre." As I have already said, both religion and theatre were in me from childhood. I pursued both interests through graduate school and on into teaching and writing. I knew that they converged, so to speak, in ritual; but my education was such that the only literature about ritual I discovered had to do with high Christian liturgy, which did not attract me because my upbringing and my theology were Low Church.

Then came the great cultural and political upheavals of the 1960s. To broaden my horizons I began to read some anthropology, where I found an approach to the study of ritual that I could use. I discovered its universality, as well as its myriad forms and social settings. In 1970 or thereabout I met Richard Schechner and began long-lasting discussions with him that in turn led me to the ideas of Victor Turner. Meanwhile, Ron Grimes, who had once studied with me, had turned his attention from literature to ritual and started something called "ritual studies." All of these things led me to pursue an enticing mix of theology, anthropology, performance studies, and religious studies.

Yet when I sat down to consider what I would say today in response to Bert Wallace's invitation, the theme threatened to wilt like yesterday's flowers. The topic seemed in peril of irrelevance. What, I asked myself, have "ritual, religion, and theatre" got to do with the lamentations and urgencies of our time?

I find *myself* these days in a state of mind close to mourning. Cry, the beloved country. Its long-term future—the future of my people, not to speak of all others' people—does not seem bright. I find myself in agreement with those many who speak of our country's decline. Its health— be it medical, social, educational, or economic—is not robust. Even the physical environment necessary to civilized life may not endure, certainly not if we continue along our present path. And there seems little will to change.

Not long before his untimely death, the late historian Tony Judt published a little book called *Ill Fares the Land*. The phrase comes from a couplet by Oliver Goldsmith: "Ill fares the land, to hastening ills a prey, / Where wealth accumulates and men decay."[3] My feelings exactly.

There is little need to enumerate America's hastening ills. I have already alluded to some of them. All seem to me symptoms or results of one underlying *dis*-ease of an ideological nature. America seems unable to give adequate address to its social problems because we are, on the whole, in the grip of an ideology of *individualism* that is increasingly at odds with the forces of nature and technology that are bringing all creatures on planet Earth ever closer together. Objectively speaking, we are in closer communication and greater interdependence than ever, but we resist this and favor combat over collaboration.

As I pondered this, I came upon what I think may be—may *perhaps* be—most relevant in the theme of "ritual, religion, and theatre" today. If the practices of theatre and religion are to be relevant, let me say, to the systemic crises of our time, those of us who lead such practices must orient our work toward something we learn from ritual studies—namely, the concept and experience of *liminality*. I will offer a few comments about this thought before sharing with you some pictures.

As is well known, the term "liminal" came into use through Arnold van Gennep in his 1908 classic, *The Rites of Passage*. He viewed such rites as having three stages: separation, liminality, and return. To name the stage that is in between the other two while belonging to neither of them, he used a derivative of the Latin word for "threshold," which is *limen*. His idea was that an initiatory rite of passage leads an initiate through a time of being no longer the old self and not yet the new one. A temporary loss of self occurs ritually in a time that is out of time, in a space that is both very specific yet also nowhere.

A generation later, Victor Turner took up this concept and saw in it the essence of ritual.[4] In my own book *Liberating Rites*, I stood on Turner's shoulders and used liminality as the second of what I called the three great gifts of ritual.[5] The first was the creation of an order or pathway to follow. The second was the creation or enhancement of community. And the third was the transformation of the status quo into a new status or condition.

When I wrote that book, I was focused mainly on transformation. The book's subtitle is "Understanding the Transformative Power of Ritual." I was mainly concerned with rebutting the very prevalent view that rituals are by nature conservative, that they serve mainly to reinforce tradition and slow down change, if not indeed to stop it. I thought that was only half of the ritual story—indeed only a third of it. Partly influenced by Schechner, I wanted my readers to view rituals as instruments of change. As a theologian in the postcolonialist world, I wanted to align Christian thought and action with the drive toward liberation that was rising all over the world.

I have not backtracked from that concern even while America has turned ever more conservative in recent years. But I see more clearly today than when I wrote the book that movements for liberation, especially in Europe and North America, are gasping for air in an ideological atmosphere that is increasingly hostile to what should rightly be called "we, the people." The ideology of individualism, often mixed with a belief that "might makes right," obscures and weakens the reality of life together.

So it may be no wonder that when I sat down to think about what to say to this symposium, a memory of theatrical magic came back from long ago.

I was twenty-five years old in 1950, a bachelor newly arrived in New York City to attend graduate school. I bought a single ticket and went alone to see Harold Clurman's production of *The Member of the Wedding* by Carson McCullers. With the rest of the audience, I was put under a spell by Ethel Waters singing "His Eye Is on the Sparrow." And later another spell at the final curtain. The play's story is about the intense desire, not to say longing, of a young girl named Frankie Addams (played by Julie Harris) to attend the forthcoming wedding of her older sister. In the last scene, the way becomes clear for her to do that, and she exclaims with joy: "The wedding will be the *we* of me." Curtain.

I will never forget what happened next. There was long applause and several curtain calls. And then we just sat there. No one wanted to leave. The strangers sitting next to me were just as immobile as I was. After a few moments we hitherto strangers began to talk to each other. The theatre had become the "we" of us. The performances onstage (and everything that Clurman and the crew did to enable them) had performed something over and above the dramatis personae roles. They had created for that brief moment in time—less brief than most such occasions—a community of people whose lives otherwise did not cross. We call it theatre magic, which means we don't quite understand it and can never predict just when it will happen. But when it does occur our joy is immense. It is like, or somehow related to, a religious experience. No matter what Kierkegaard had to say.

In an age in which the term "public" has been denigrated in favor of "privatization," when housing is increasingly "gated" if it is affordable at all, when public education and health care and transportation and all manner of intrinsically social services are either neglected or attacked as impingements upon "liberty," when guns are thought to be necessary almost everywhere in the name of self-defense—in such a time, the liminality of theatre and ritual and yes, worship if it is truly communitarian, becomes vitally important.

I'm suggesting that theatre practitioners and arrangers of ritual alike should keep their eyes on the prize of liminality and not let themselves be satisfied with attention to the frameworks of method and technique on the one hand, or with message and manifest content on the other.

There is no technique that can assure the experience of liminality. In the church we say that it is accomplished by prayer and attentiveness to the Spirit. In the theatre, I think it is much the same, although the vocabulary may be different. I think of something once said by the Haitian artist and Vodou practitioner André Pierre: "The world is created by magic. . . . No one lives of the flesh. Everyone lives of the spirit."

To illustrate what I'm trying to say, I will share a few pictures from Haiti, a land rich in ritual where I learned a great deal about the topic. I will show some images of scenes that I have previously discussed only in words—in chapter 4 of *Liberating Rites*, a chapter called "Priest and Shaman: Two Pathways of Religious Ritual."[6]

Figure 1. Inside Les Cayes Cathedral. Photo by author.

We are in the Roman Catholic cathedral at Les Cayes, a town on Haiti's southern coast. A service is being held for the ordination of seven new priests. I call your attention to the familiar architecture:

- the long, straight nave, leading up to the high altar in the distance;
- the tall arches, with their emphasis upon verticality—high versus low.

The architectural layout of Christian churches is derived from what the Romans called a basilica, which was a court building. In this tradition, to be in church is to be in court, paying homage to God, the judge who looks down from above.

Figure 2. Enthroning the bishop. Photo by author.

The whole idea here is the display of authority—the authority of God transmitted through the authority of the bishop and the clergy. In this picture, the miter of authority is placed on the bishop's head.

Figure 3. Obeisance. Photo by author.

After taking vows of obedience, the new priests lie prostrate before the bishop.

Figure 4. Clergy here, laity there. Photo by author.

Take notice of the sharp divide between clergy and laity. On the right, the priests stand as if on a shoreline facing away from the vast sea of lay people behind them. There is contact between the two groups only later during the act of communion, but even then there is no mingling.

Figure 5. *Poteau mitan*. Photo by author.

And now this. We are in a *hounfo*, or worship space. It has two primary architectural features:

- a decorated center pole, called a *poteau mitan*, and
- a beaten-earth floor.

There may be other decorations, but only these two are essential.

The model for a *servis vodou* is not that of a court, as it is in the traditional church layout. Instead, what we're having is a sacred party. At the first such event that I ever attended in Haiti, I turned to my wife and asked, "What does this seem like to you?" And she answered what I was already thinking: "It feels like Saturday night." Indeed. Sometimes the *houngan* or *mambo* will send out engraved invitations, inviting the recipients to a party to honor one of the many spirits, or *lwa*.

Figure 6. Paying respect. Photo by author.

The poteau mitan is one of several "points" in the room that may become entryways for the visiting spirits. Early in the service homage is paid to each of these, as well as to any specially honored human guests. Then the party moves on. Notice that reverence is given to the *foot* of the pole, not to its height, for the foot is where the spirits' presence will be felt.

Figure 7. Movement. Photo by author.

There is constant movement. Instead of verticality and straight lines, here we have circularity in motion. Although the poteau mitan is vertical, the action, mostly dancing, goes on around it. Nobody looks *up*. Everything moves *around*.

Anthropologists call this type of religion *ecstatic*.[7] Drumming, singing, dancing, and a certain amount of rum produce sensory overload. Some of the participants go into trance or spirit-possession.

The drumming itself, let alone all the rest, can send you off. Back in New York after my research in Haiti, I sat at my desk one morning listening with headphones to my recordings of a *servis*. It was all drumming and singing. After about an hour of this I took a break. Walking down the hall to get some coffee, I realized that I was high as a kite. Oh, those drums! It's not for nothing that the Haitians baptize them and give them personal names.

Figure 8. *Houngan* in red (right) with woman in blue. Photo by author.

The man on the right is the houngan, who has been possessed by a spirit called Simbi. Now he has a double role. As houngan, he is the host of the party. Like a good host, he is always *among* the people and almost never in the *center*. At the same time, possessed by Simbi, he wears Simbi's costume and delivers advice and counsel to several people, including this woman. Notice the close contact between them; and notice her attitude of intense listening to a figure whom she sees as a divine guest of honor.

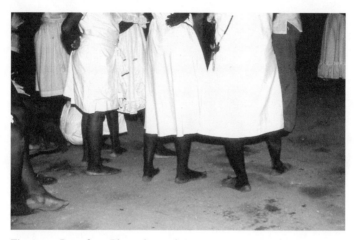

Figure 9. Bare feet. Photo by author.

No shoes. The worshippers' bare feet must make contact with the earthen floor.

Figure 10. Dancing girl with *asson*. Photo by author.

Above all, there is constant motion. Once started, the drumming does not stop, nor does the singing and dancing.

Figure 11. Ceremonial movement. Photo by author.

The ceremonial movement is equally dance-like.

Figure 12. No one center. Photo by author.

We can say that the focus of the cathedral ritual is upon order. This is not to say that it has no element of liminality, but the latter is greatly subordinate to the former. The designers and leaders of such ritual want us to follow—to follow the "order" of service, as it is sometimes called (in Latin the *ordo*); to follow church teachings and doctrines; to follow the bishop, and the bishop of bishops, the Pope; and to follow God, which in this case is the same thing.

By contrast, the focus of the hounfo ritual is—well, we have a problem. This ritual is relatively *unfocused*. There is no center. That is to say, no *fixed* center. There are multiple centers—centers of attention that move and change, occurrences or happenings that come and go.

Figure 13. *Vevé.* Photo by author.

Consider this emblem, called a *vevé*. At the beginning of a servis, after the drumming and singing have begun, the vevé is drawn on the earthen floor with cornmeal. It takes some skill; and it is quite wonderful to see the design emerge beneath the hand of the artisan while the drums beat. Each divine spirit has a particular vevé design. It is put on the floor to create a *point* through which that spirit may enter the room and take part in the goings-on.

During the service this carefully wrought design will disappear. It will be rubbed out by the feet of the dancing worshippers.

Things come and go. The spirits themselves come and go. You hold a servis (that is, give a party) for *this* one and instead *that* one shows up. Or they both show up and one gets rowdy and has to be told to leave. A possession occurs unpredictably. The possessed one's body jerks, twitches, perhaps falls to the floor. A few people gather around to make sure there is no bodily injury. It's a normal occurrence, so it interrupts nothing. The party goes on. Perhaps another possession occurs soon in another part of the room. The drumming never stops until the party is over. It may last five or six hours. Who cares what time it is?

I come now to an important double point about liminality—namely its *transcendence* and its *transience*. Liminality does not belong to things, nor to persons, nor to any fixed places, nor to any set times. In theological language we might say that its time is that of *kairos* rather than *chronos*.

Those of us who have been brought up in sacramental religions such as traditional Christianity are tempted to think that certain objects are sacred in and of themselves—the sacramental bread and wine, the saint's relic, a piece of the Cross, or whatever. Even as a Bible Belt Protestant, I was brought up to hold the church "sanctuary," as we called it, in awe, even when it was empty on weekdays.

Galway Kinnell once wrote a contemplative poem about Avenue C in Manhattan, in which he coined a marvelous phrase. As he watched the avenue's lights turning on and off while the traffic moved and twilight came, he said that he experienced "instants of transcendence." We could also call these liminal moments.

Figure 14. Man holding up *asson*. Photo by author.

The man is a houngan taking part in a servis. The object he holds is an *asson*, a hollowed-out gourd wrapped with plastic beads that turn it into a rattle. In former times, the beads were the vertebrae of snakes, but that was then.

With the asson, the houngan or mambo conducts the servis. He signals to the drummers when to change rhythms and what rhythms to use. He signals to the lwa to come hither, or to behave themselves, or whatever. This is his instrument as the master of ceremonies, which means the host of the party, which means the arranger of events that are all designed to make way for "instants of transcendence." We can, if we like, speak of this as a sacred object.

Figure 15. Baby playing with *asson*. Photo by author.

But it is not sacred all of the time. When the servis is not happening, the asson can become a child's toy. It doesn't matter. We are not concerned with *things* but with what might be called "divine happenings."

I have one more picture sequence to share with you, also from Haiti. Its purpose is to show the link that can occur between performance and transcendence. This is a story about a woman who prayed in front of the camera.

Figure 16. Many people in waterfall. Photo by author.

Every summer in the mountains of Haiti there is a festival called Saut d'Eau, which means waterfall. It is a festival of cleansing. Pilgrims come from all over Haiti to this cascade, where the main thing is to go into the water and wash away all the sins and mistakes and bad fortune that have clung to you. I went in myself and felt like a child again.

Figure 17. Candles burning at tree base. Photo by author.

Near the waterfall are some large, sacred trees. That is, the trees be-come sacred by virtue of the fact that people come to them and burn candles and offer prayers.

Figure 18. Saut d'Eau—Woman at prayer. Photo by author.

I was just sitting and watching things when this woman, whom I did not know, began to pray while looking up into the tree. I knew that Dam-ballah, the snake spirit, lives in trees.

Figure 19. Saut d'Eau—Woman at prayer. Photo by author.

I watched and listened as she prayed fervently. But I could not understand her because I do not speak Kreyol. When she stopped, my assistant came over and told me what she had prayed. She and her son had a small farm on land that was claimed by a big landowner. Last year he sent thugs who kidnapped her son and killed him. She stayed on the farm. Now the bad guys have returned and are trying to seize her land. She is praying for protection and for justice.

I was so moved that I asked to speak to her. I gave her a blessing, and then I asked her if she would mind praying again in front of my camera. She agreed, and the next thing I knew, she was praying once again.

I was both amazed and fascinated when her praying the second time through, and with the explicit purpose of my taking her picture, turned out to be at least as fervent as the first time, if not more.

Theatre persons who work daily with live performances and rehearsals will recognize this phenomenon. There is an ambiguity that is inherent in the very words "perform" and "act." Both words mean both to do and to pretend. In any actual performance, liminal transcendence can come and go.

In this woman's case, it came and went and came again. Whatever self-consciousness the camera may have induced, it was swept away by the urgency of her situation and her need.

Let me end this presentation by returning to our own needs. There are in our country many specific needs that are urgent at the present time—among them better health care, better education, better transportation, better physical infrastructure, more and better jobs, affordable housing of a certain standard, and on and on and on. Taken together, they will jeopardize our future if not adequately addressed.

But there is also what I think of as a spiritual need. By this I do not mean more religion but better religion. By the same token, I mean something that many people would not think of as religious at all. I mean a renewal of appreciation of our life together as human beings.

I am not talking about feelings of chumminess or clubbiness. I am talking about a sense of loyalty and devotion to humankind as such. It includes large amounts of understanding and compassion. It includes a passion for justice.

And it is not just in the head. It is also in the hands and the feet. It is not merely ideational but also performative. That is why ritual and theatre and the action component of religion are so crucial. People in the performing arts, and people in charge of ritual life, which is also performative, have a high calling. It is, if I may put it in the simplest of terms, to bring us together. That is why I have talked about liminality.

We should remember that liminality is not a stable resting place. It is transient. It is achieved or experienced momentarily. It cannot even be directly planned. But it can be prepared for. We can clear the way for it if we realize that what we are after is not the same as our means of arranging for it. In short, we must do our work in a spirit of openness to a reality of spirit that we cannot control.

Finally, a caveat. Liminality does not solve ethical problems. Saint Paul advised the churches to "test the spirits, to see whether they be of God." Not all spirits are good ones. The togetherness of liminality can easily be transformed into the mass psychology of totalitarianism, or into an orgy of consumerism, or the fever of war. When I taught a course on rituals and sacraments, I always included a screening of Leni Riefenstahl's *Triumph of the Will* in order to show that not all ritual is beneficent, however seductive and self-transcending it may be.

Values and rationality do matter. I hope nothing I have said leads to the conclusion that they do not. But they are neither the end of the matter nor the heart of the matter. "Everyone lives of the spirit." Whether we are arrangers of ritual, practitioners of religion, or workers in theatre, our task is to serve and invoke the highest spirit that we know.

Notes

1. James P. Carse, *The Religious Case against Belief* (New York: Penguin, 2008).

2. Cf. *Waiting for Godot*.

3. Oliver Goldsmith, *The Deserted Village*, 1770. Quoted in Tony Judt, *Ill Fares the Land* (New York: Penguin, 2010).

4. Victor Turner, *The Ritual Process: Structure and Anti-Structure* (1969; repr. Baltimore: Penguin Books, 1974; 1969).

5. Tom F. Driver, *Liberating Rites: Understanding the Transformative Power of Ritual* (Amazon / CreateSpace, 2006; HarperSanFrancisco, 1991, as *The Magic of Ritual*). See especially part 3, "Ritual's Social Gifts," 133–94.

6. Ibid., 52–78.

7. See I. M. Lewis, *Ecstatic Religion: A Study of Shamanism and Spirit Possession*, 2nd ed. (New York: Routledge, 1989).

Transferring Belief

The Stage Presence of the Spiritual Meme

Cohen Ambrose

A S PERFORMANCE practitioners, we hear a lot about the so-called power of theatre. Yet not all live performances are powerful. So when they are, what makes them so? This essay uses the neuroscience of spectating and imitation to make the argument that live performance has the ability to transfer certain units of cultural information—including those with spiritual content—from performer to spectator. These transferable units, called memes, can be as specific as a simple melody or as sophisticated and individualized as a spiritual belief system. I am interested in how certain units of spiritual ideology can be spread from character to spectator in the theatre. It is important for us as artists to consider the biological impact of the transmission of ideas from the stage space to the audience.

In *The Selfish Gene*, Richard Dawkins coined the controversial term *meme*, an abbreviation of the Greek root *mimema*, "to imitate." Dawkins uses the term to define units of culture including "tunes, ideas, catch-phrases, clothes fashions, ways of making pots or of building arches."[1] Just as genes are passed on from parents to children, memes, Dawkins argues, can be passed on from brain to brain via cultural transmission. This transmission takes place via the subconscious imitation of the behavior of others and through formal and informal education. Susan Blackmore similarly argues that memes, like genes, evolve by "memetic selection." She also suggests that religious memes eventually have an impact on which genes are successful.[2]

In *Breaking the Spell*, cognitive philosopher Daniel Dennett argues that we should "set aside our traditional reluctance to investigate religious phenomena scientifically, so that we can come to understand how and why religions inspire such devotion."[3] He argues that religion is such an influential natural phenomenon that it must be understood in order to make informed political decisions. I would argue that as performance practitioners, we benefit from understanding the science of spiritual belief systems in order to make informed aesthetic decisions.

In the past decade, theatre scholarship has crossed disciplinary lines with the cognitive sciences to better understand how spectators become engaged with the subject matter represented on the stage. In *Engaging Audiences*, Bruce McConachie examines how various cultural concepts, empathy, and emotion are working in the minds of spectators during a theatrical performance. He argues that the cognitive sciences can tell us, as theatre practitioners, how to better understand and stimulate the spectator's brain. He writes: "As actors and spectators, we want to be pushed to emotional extremes," and so "audiences must engage with actors . . . and the artists . . . must engage with the spectators."[4] Using recent neurological research concerning imitation, McConachie argues that while witnessing a staged event, the brain itself imitates the event, thereby effectively experiencing it. In other words, what the senses perceive, the brain translates into actual experience on the neuronal level. Once the spectator's brain has simulated the experience of the event onstage, a unit of cultural information—a meme—has been transferred.

Building on McConachie's argument, I suggest that the brain, through a series of cognitive and psychosomatic processes, has the capacity to share in the representation of spiritual experiences onstage. Theatrical performances can act as neurological rehearsals for real-life scenarios, forming new neural pathways that create or reinforce belief in specific spiritual ideologies. Performative representations of spiritual experiences can, like the genetic code found in our DNA, carry and transmit elements of spiritual culture.

In *Mystical Mind*, Eugene d'Aquili and Andrew B. Newberg explore a possible evolutionary development of the brain that includes spiritual experience. They define the "cognitive imperative" as people's inherent need to "organize their world cognitively" and to "use their rational mind/brain to wonder about God and the mysteries of religion."[5] The process of witnessing the representation of a spiritual experience onstage encourages the development of new neural pathways that make room for a cognitive organization of the unseen world.

The notion that the human brain—indeed, the mind itself—and the human body are interconnected is substantiated by consistent discoveries by neuroscientists. Humans undergo most motor development after birth. Unlike ungulates and other large mammals that can walk moments after birth, humans are effectively helpless as newborns. We learn motor skills by watching others perform them. Because infants cannot physically perform the tasks they are attempting to imitate, they are really imitating the *intent* of the task. As infants develop the ability to embody some of these goal-oriented tasks, they begin to link the intent to a specific meaning. As the meaning becomes clear, McConachie suggests, these mental mirror systems of imitation begin to "link . . . to the general dynamics of cultural learning, maintenance, and change."[6] Our brains develop in such a way that by first imitating physical actions, we develop an understanding of intent, which then informs how we perceive social processes. The ability to "read" another's physical behavior is an evolutionary trait that allows humans to make quick judgments about social status and risk of threat.

Neuroscience research is showing that the performance of tasks learned by imitating others is a physical phenomenon unique to humans and select species of monkeys. In the mid-1990s, a team of neuroscientists led by Giacomo Rizzolatti at the University of Parma, Italy, working with macaque monkeys, discovered what is now called the "mirror effect," or mirror neurons. Mirror neuron systems make up about 20 percent of the brain's neurons in some monkeys and humans. These systems contain a concentration of neurons that teach the brain how to perform basic tasks by imitating others. When we observe someone else reach for a glass of water, for example, the same network of neurons begins to fire as if we were reaching for the glass of water ourselves. Not only do the observer and the performer have the same neuronal experience, but the observer can also read the difference between whether the performer is reaching for the glass for a drink or to clear the table. Marco Iacoboni, one of the Parma scientists, calls this the "ideomotor model of human actions," which "assumes that the starting point of human actions are the *intentions* associated with them, and that actions should be mostly considered as a means to achieve those intentions."[7] This is significant because the brain behaves as if the body is actually physically performing the task. A single active neuron can simultaneously code for an action (grasping the glass) as well as a perception (observing the grasp).[8]

The ability to predict the intentions of another—whether of others in real life or of a character onstage—is the direct scientific link between the performer and the spectator. Because we make direct links between physical behavior and psychological intent during the process of imitation, we cannot consider this process without implicating the role the physical body plays in live performance. McConachie suggests that our main avenue of connection to the characters onstage is through physically determined intentions because "our mirror systems bridge actor-audience communication where intentional physical movement is concerned."[9] Similarly, as Iacoboni points out, imitation processes are located in the motor and movement areas of the neocortex. Therefore, he writes, "it makes little theoretical sense to think about the imitation process in general, abstract terms without considering the body parts and type of actions involved."[10] In other words, humans cannot read one another's minds, but we can attempt to read one another's bodies and predict the intentions of one another's minds. This may be effective on a basic level, for example, to determine whether or not another is a threat. But to assume that a body is telling the truth about its mental processes is not always reliable. This is where live performance becomes so significant: it addresses phenomenological intersubjectivity, an experience we all have every day.

Intersubjectivity is the sharing of significance and meaning between individuals. By observing the embodied expression of emotion in others, we register what they are feeling before we can even describe their specific body language. While this all happens on a prereflective level, Iacoboni argues that mirror neurons allow humans to have interconnected social interactions between one another. He maintains that this interdependence creates a "concrete encounter between self and other [that] becomes the shared existential meaning that connects them deeply."[11]

As the human brain's use of mirror neuron systems creates a neuronal copy of the observed action of another, it can also use simulation and imagination, or motor imagery, to have the desired neuronal experience. Again, by imagining ourselves performing a physical task or having a specific type of psychophysical experience, we are having the same neuronal experience as we would if we were actually physically performing the action. Shortly after the experiments at Parma, for example, neuroscientist Jean Decety published a paper in which he examines whether or not the timing of mentally simulated actions correlates with actual physically performed actions. Using mental chronometry—measuring the brain's response time to a stimulus under both actual and imagined circumstances—Decety found that subjects mentally responded to a stimulus in the same amount of time as if they were physically experiencing it. "Motor imagery," he writes, "can be defined as a dynamic state during which a subject mentally simulates a given action. This type of phenomenal experience implies that the subject feels himself performing a given action."[12]

The theatre is a space that allows experiments that encourage the expansion of cognitive organization through symbolic representation and the projection of metaphors. Reading the physicality of the characters onstage helps spectators shape subsequent cognitive processes in such a way that they begin to generate symbolic social meaning about the characters. For example, if performers kneel, clasp their hands at their chest, close their eyes, and begin to murmur softly, prayer immediately comes to mind. A prayer posture or gesture is an image that is translatable and universally recognizable. Iacoboni argues that by tapping into the minds of others via the symbolism of their physicality, "our brains are capable of accessing other minds by using the neural mechanisms of . . . simulation."[13] By mentally simulating a spiritual experience through the observance of another's (real or staged) concrete experience, an individual is potentially able to construct his or her own spiritual encounter.

The ending of part I of Tony Kushner's *Angels in America, Part One* is arguably one of the most spectacular recent examples of spiritual encounter in American playwriting. To witness the actor, dressed as an angel and suspended from visible wires, come bursting through Prior's bedroom ceiling is a blatant staging of a spiritual meme. Kushner does not use the image to promote any kind of spiritual or religious ideology but rather appropriates an iconic religious meme in order to make a specific comment on historical and current tensions between gay and religious communities in the United States. Though the spectator knows it is not a "real" angel, Kushner asks the audience to join the actor performing the role of Prior in mentally simulating a spiritual encounter. Allowing oneself to suspend disbelief in order to simulate extraordinary phenomena is perhaps driven by a need to reify experiences that do not conform to everyday physical limitation.

In their book, d'Aquili and Newberg coin the term *neurotheology*. They examine the neurophysiology of theological thought processes and experiences. They explain that they are not exploring any one type of spiritual structure; rather, they hope to develop a kind of "metatheology that does not have specific theological content, but explains the essential components of any specific theology."[14] They argue that the cognitive imperative and the activity of specific cognitive operators are why humans create spiritual structures in the first place. The authors propose that when humans have witnessed a spiritual event—real, imagined, or simulated onstage—the cognitive imperative "takes over such that we have the burning desire to understand what the experience actually represented."[15] As the name implies, the cognitive imperative derives from our rational brain, which relies on organization and an intense need to make sense of otherwise abstract experiences. The need to attach symbolic meaning to such events comes from the desire to reify the experience, and, the authors conclude, there is thus "a strong emotional drive to explore the ultimate since these are perhaps the most emotional states that can be achieved."[16] If spiritual experiences are indeed the most emotional states humans access, the more powerful the representation of the experience, the more "spiritual" neurons are created.

This process of organization that we seem to need in order to make sense of the world requires exercise. This "mental fitness routine" is possible due to *neuroplasticity*. Just as our muscles are malleable and able to expand and contract, our brains need stimulation in order to form new neural pathways and operate effectively in real-life thought situations. Just as we rehearse a scene in a play to exercise our memory, we need to perform the scene's text and movements and rehearse thought processes in order to form new neural connections. What we observe in others, we experience ourselves on a neural level, and so we exercise the connections between those regions of the brain involved in the experience. Neuro-scientist Daniel Siegel explains in his book *Mindsight* that "when we focus our attention in specific ways, we create neural firing patterns that permit previously separated areas to become linked and integrated."[17] Thus, the cognitive imperative encourages our brains to make symbolic, empathetic, and representational connections between what they are observing and potential future scenarios. Using the imitative capabilities of our brains while observing a simulation of a spiritual encounter encourages the development of neural pathways dedicated to facilitating spiritual experiences.

While concepts of cultural transmission and evolution date clear back to the early nineteenth century, the actual definition of a unit of culture is relatively new. Dawkins's theory has been embraced by some and disregarded as unscientific by many. While geneticists can measure and define specific genes by the structure of DNA strands and their particular subunits of nucleotides, it is impossible to measure memes. An evolutionary biologist himself, Dawkins essentially builds his idea on an analogy: genes are to hereditary evolution as memes are to cultural evolution. He seeks to organize and examine the process by which ideas are passed on from individual to individual and spread throughout social structures. Because humans are able to adopt, copy, and reproduce ideas brain-to-brain via the subconscious imitation of ideas, the potential power of live theatre in the transmission of spiritual ideology is significant. The proliferation of spiritual ideology is so effective that the memes associated with religion may even drive the positive evolution of genes for religious behavior.

In *The Meme Machine*, Susan Blackmore argues that there is a correlation between the evolution of mass religions and the evolution of certain genes. By tracing archaeological discoveries of jewelry buried with remains of the dead, Blackmore makes the case that *Homo sapiens* developed some idea of an afterlife nearly fifty thousand years ago.[18] "Brain development," she writes, "is under genetic control and it is known that some brains are more prone to religious belief and experience than others."[19] She argues that people with damaged or unstable temporal lobes—the region of the brain responsible for the development of long-term memory, perception, and recognition—are more prone to reporting supernatural experiences. Blackmore suggests that religious memes are "stored, and thus given improved longevity, in the great religious texts." She argues that the Bible is deserving of the accolade "survival of the fittest" because it actually gives the instruction to pass its ideas on. The Bible, Blackmore writes, "is extremely adaptable, and since much of its content is self-contradictory it can be used to justify more or less any action or moral stance."[20] Perhaps because religious texts are such successful memes in themselves, plays and theatrical performances often incorporate elements of their stories and characters. Just as memes can generate the proliferation of successful genes, memes also take over after the hereditary process has done its work.

As we now know, the process of witnessing the physical representation of a spiritual encounter is, on the neurological level, just the same as if the spectator were physically experiencing it. If there is indeed an evolutionary need for—and perhaps advantage to—articulating a spiritual organization of the universe, then perhaps the theatre can help encourage this process on the neural level. Dawkins argues that once the brain has done its work in developing an empathetic response via imitation, culture takes the wheel and promotes the distribution of the most beneficial memes. He suggests that after the genetic transmission of biological traits occurs, the brain is equipped to learn through imitation. Then, culture takes over.[21]

Like d'Aquili and Newberg, Dawkins guesses that for some reason, the highly infectious "god meme" must be in the brain's best interest. He argues that "the survival value of the god meme in the meme pool results from its great psychological appeal" and that in order to rectify the confusion of a chaotic world, "it provides a superficially plausible answer to deep and troubling questions about existence."[22] He goes on to suggest that the god meme "is none the less effective for being imaginary."[23] I agree. Based on what we know about the neurological parallels between the experienced and the imagined, it is plausible that the reason the transference of a spiritual meme (mono- or polytheistic) is so successful is that it satisfies our cognitive imperative to attach symbolic meaning to our existence. Even if God is completely imaginary, the brain behaves as if he is real.

D'Aquili and Newberg explain with neuroscience what Dawkins cannot, because without the use of modern technology (such as functional magnetic resonance imaging), Dawkins is merely guessing. For him, viewing the organization of the universe as including an ultimate being is irrational. He concludes his chapter on the meme by arguing that the propagation of the idea of God throughout culture is a collective attempt to escape the complexities of rational, scientific thought. He argues that "the meme for blind faith secures its own perpetuation by the simple unconscious expedient of discouraging rational inquiry."[24] In other words, because the world is chaotic, random, and violent, humans look for something reliable and static to guide them through it. However, if we accept d'Aquili and Newberg's assertion that the cognitive imperative is a neurological necessity, Dawkins's argument that humans prefer blind faith over rational inquiry no longer applies. In fact, it is precisely because of the brain's need to rely on rational inquiry that humans have created so many complex spiritual structures that all attempt to explain our existence.

Spiritual memes can be elements of religious dogma: in Roman Catholicism, for example, the Pope speaks the word of God and wine literally becomes the blood of Christ. They can be highly individualized beliefs about the supernatural. Whatever form they take, these individual units of spiritual culture that make up entire religions and belief systems can be transferred from brain to brain. The spiritual memes within a live performance in a theatre space, around a fire, in a Greek amphitheater, in a church, or in a school, are copied, translated in various forms from brain to brain, and distributed around the space. This kind of spiritual give-and-take has a special stage presence because it is inextricably linked to an evolutionary need to organize the unseen world.

Our brains have the ability to instinctually make decisions about what our values are. Usually, these value and belief systems come from our parents. As we develop, we may or may not begin to shift our beliefs and the values associated with them. As Newberg points out in *Why We Believe What We Believe*, "Our brains are instinctually prone to reject information that does not conform to our prior experience and knowledge."[25]

Pinning down a firm set of beliefs and values is an evolutionary trait. As d'Aquili and Newberg make clear, it is imperative that our cognitive understanding of the world include a symbolic representation of the ultimate meaning of existence (including the scientific) if we are to function within our given social structure. If this is the case, then it is reasonable that individuals want to pass on to their children and other fellow humans that same sense of security or plausible answer to all the mysteries in life. It is clear, based on what we know about the way our brains develop, that infants and children imitate others in order to gain information about the new world in which they exist.

While humans are born with many mammalian instincts, we learn the meaning behind our impulses after birth. It is because of this that we have mirror neuron systems that help us learn new skills from one another. Just as we learn new and valuable physical skills by imitation, we also learn valuable ideas and concepts by the imitation of others' belief systems. Therefore, performance practitioners must be aware of the power of the spiritual meme. Every emotion a spectator experiences while engaging with the intentions of a character onstage will create new ways of thinking. As the spectator feels a specific emotion—even in a prereflective way—all other cognitive operations rewire themselves to support the experience of that emotion. This rewiring process creates fertile pathways within which religious and spiritual memes can flourish. "In other words," McConachie writes, "emotions generated through simulation change the way people think."[26] As we rise to a level of awareness of the science of performance, spectating, and imitation, we have the opportunity to adjust the ways in which we stage highly emotional and spiritual encounters. It is vital that as performance practitioners, we take responsibility for the spiritual memes we place onstage and consciously align their impact with our objectives.

Notes

1. Richard Dawkins, *The Selfish Gene*, 30th anniversary ed. (Oxford: Oxford University Press, 2006), 192.

2. Susan Blackmore, *The Meme Machine* (Oxford: Oxford University Press, 1999), 14.

3. Daniel Dennett, *Breaking the Spell: Religion as a Natural Phenomenon* (New York: Penguin, 2007), 26.

4. Bruce McConachie, *Engaging Audiences: A Cognitive Approach to Spectating in the Theatre* (New York: Palgrave Macmillan, 2008), 1.

5. Eugene d'Aquili and Andrew B. Newberg, *Mystical Mind: Probing the Biology of Religious Experience* (Minneapolis: Fortress, 1999), 164.

6. McConachie, *Engaging Audiences*, 77.

7. Marco Iacoboni, *Mirroring People* (New York: Farrar, Straus and Giroux, 2008), 58.

8. Ibid., 22.

9. McConachie, *Engaging Audiences*, 74.

10. Marco Iacoboni, "Neurobiology of Imitation," *Neurobiology of Behavior* 19 (2009): 662.

11. Iacoboni, *Mirroring People*, 265.

12. Jean Decety, "Do Imagined and Executed Actions Share the Same Neural Substrate?" *Cognitive Brain Research* 3, no. 2 (1996): 87.

13. Iacoboni, *Mirroring People*, 264.

14. D'Aquili and Newberg, *Mystical Mind*, 163.

15. Ibid., 165.

16. Ibid.

17. Daniel Siegel, *Mindsight* (New York: Bantam, 2010), 43.

18. Blackmore, *Meme Machine*, 195.

19. Ibid., 197.

20. Ibid., 192.

21. Dawkins, *Selfish Gene*, 200.

22. Ibid., 193.

23. Ibid.

24. Ibid., 198.

25. Andrew B. Newberg, *Why We Believe What We Believe* (New York: Free Press, 2006), 6.

26. McConachie, *Engaging Audiences*, 69.

Ritual Performance and Spirituality in the Work of The Living Theatre, Past and Present

David Callaghan

T HE EXPERIMENTAL theatre of the 1960s, often inspired by the theories of Antonin Artaud, generally abandoned traditional dramatic structure and literary masterpieces in favor of ensemble-driven, ritualistic work rooted in the body that sought to transcend the limits of verbal, cognitive-based communication. While important work was done by companies led by Peter Brook, Jerzy Grotowski, Richard Schechner, Joseph Chaikin, and others, Julian Beck and Judith Malina's troupe the Living Theatre occupies a singular, long-lasting, and significant position in this theatrical landscape. In my essay, I will explore how the Living Theatre, initially as part of the larger 1960s radical theatre movement, sought to merge art and life and create a performance space that could allow for spiritual transcendence. In a sense, those who seek out the Living Theatre have a spiritual intention that resonates with the altruistic intent of their ensemble-driven work. (I have experienced this firsthand, having sought out the company after seeing *Tablets* in 1989 while still a graduate student, which eventually led to my work with Reznikov as assistant director on *Rules of Civility* in 1991.) The Living Theatre essentially used performance, including extensive audience participation, as a contemporary act of secular ritual that could provide spiritual sustenance to a decaying culture it believed needed new myths and rites of worship. The Living Theatre is also unique in its long-standing commitment to this spiritual mission, and it is still active today. The company continues to negotiate how daily life might intersect with the theatre as a holy space of sorts, where visions of a richer, spiritual world and human existence can be forged in performance first among a company and then between actors and spectators.

Founded in 1947 by Beck and Malina as part of the off-Broadway movement, the Living Theatre by the early 1960s was most interested in awakening what it perceived as a passive, spiritually alienated audience. Frequently, its experiments were rooted in myth and ritual harkening back to the origins of theatre as a means of restoring a sense of vitality and importance to contemporary performance. Beck conceived their theatre as an encounter "that would be an intense experience halfway between dreams and rituals, through which the spectator could achieve intimate comprehension of himself . . . and the nature of things."[1] Beck further described the appeal of Artaud for the Living, as they are referred to in Europe, in "his desire to bring to the theatre the outcry, the great scream, as the Greeks tried to reach for that moment of scream. It was the protest, the way at least of the voice breaking out of the inhibition. Do I dare and raise my voice? . . . Artaud wanted to smash the whole prison society with that outcry, with that scream."[2]

Numerous other artists challenged rigid and often authoritarian conventions and institutions in this period. In general, the avant-garde theatre of the 1960s envisioned the theatrical encounter as a means of forging new communities and more authentic value systems for both artists and spectators. While different companies created their own style of theatre, certain characteristics emerged in common during this era. Because of the influence of Artaud and his Theatre of Cruelty, traditional dialogue and characters were typically abandoned in favor of sound and movement rooted in ensemble collaboration. Artists rejected naturalism in favor of seeking the metaphysical in Artaudian "speech, gesture and expression." Theatre pieces were often created around a series of rituals, frequently involving audience participation. As critic Margaret Croyden noted, "Artaud set the tone for the radical theater of the sixties. . . . What he envisioned . . . was a ritual theatre, of psychotherapy and spiritual transformation."[3] Richard Schechner, founder of The Performance Group and editor of the *Drama Review* during this period, argued that ritual and theatre differed significantly within boundaries of performance. For Schechner, conventional theatre offered entertainment for a passive, separate audience, whereas ritual allowed for the spectator to engage in participatory acts that could create a community with transformative potential. The work of social scientist Victor Turner later influenced Schechner's work in the area of performance studies, with Turner's notion of the liminal defined as a place "neither here nor there," but rather "betwixt and between the positions assigned and arrayed by law, custom, convention and ceremony."[4] For Schechner, in the liminal phase of ritual two essential things occur: those undergoing the ritual are temporarily "put into a state of extreme vulnerability where they are open to change . . . in the midst of a journey from one social self to another. Second . . . persons are inscribed with their new identities and initiated into their new powers."[5] The liminal phase allows for the possibility of creating new situations, personal identities, and social constructs. Ritualistic actions and symbolic objects signify its conclusion, and "each marks the transformation that is taking place."[6] Turner employed the term "liminoid" in modern cultures to describe how the need for obligatory, sacred ritual was often taken over by voluntary, ritual-like leisure activities such as sports and popular entertainment. Schechner contends that Turner viewed aspects of the 1960s counterculture as "an attempt to recuperate the force and unity of traditional liminality."[7]

The Living Theatre was perhaps the most explicitly political theatre company of this period, and unique in its longevity and ongoing commitment to its anarchist-pacifist ideology and ongoing goal of using theatre to create its often-stated "beautiful non-violent revolution" through the present day. For Malina, anarchy has a spiritual impact, offering "a more reasonable way of organizing society. It's a form of organization that doesn't approve of violence, of hierarchy, and it's a kind of very optimistic view that we can organize our lives without punitive laws." While the Living Theatre's style of audience interaction has varied over the decades, its mission has always been aimed at effecting a deeply entrenched change in the very fabric of human interaction, behavior, and consciousness: "a change in attitude, who we are to each other, what we mean to each other, and how we should treat each other as human beings."[8]

In the late 1960s, the company decided to engage audiences directly by generating several collectively created productions that toured the United States beginning in 1968. *Mysteries and Smaller Pieces* and *Paradise Now* were structured especially as contemporary rituals with the goal of incorporating spectators into the performance and empowering them to question the status quo. *Mysteries*, the first of these works, premiered overseas in 1964 as a free-form collage of various sound-and-movement exercises, yoga postures, agitprop sketches, and improvised lighting and music. It included an enactment of Artaud's essay *The Theatre and the Plague*, followed by a gathering of the company members' bodies into a ritualistic, macabre pile. At many performances throughout the 1960s, audience members often joined the body pile as a statement of communal solidarity against the Vietnam War. The multitiered *Paradise Now*, with eight rungs consisting of multiple "rites," was especially controversial, most likely a result of several improvisatory sections that often contained nudity and profanity, where the spectators essentially created the text of the play in tandem with the company.[9] In *TDR*, Patrick McDermott responded to *Mysteries* as "unique rites of the Living Theatre, based upon their own adapted mythology" and noted *Paradise Now*'s resemblance to Old-Time Religion: "when you 'get it,' you stand up and shout and roll about. Such enthusiasm . . . can seem funny to you if you watch it. But if you try it you risk conversion, because it's fun. Physically celebratory religion is one way to make yourself feel whole. . . . Old times aside, there is an analogy between a performance of The Living Theatre and a religious service of even the most cerebral sort."[10]

Similarly, Richard Schechner described the approach of *Paradise Now* as reminding him of a Yom Kippur service, likening the audience to the congregation and the Living's actors to rabbis and cantors invested in guiding the service. Given the company's desire for the performance to end with a collective euphoria that would lead the audience out of the theatre to demand "Paradise Now," the production was perhaps the ultimate demonstration of its reliance on audience or community engagement through the liberated body at that time. Schechner has argued that people are often swept away or even "taken over" while experiencing rituals or in a liminal state. Turner referred to this "liberation from the constraints of ordinary life" as "anti-structure" and the experience of "ritual camaraderie" as "communitas." In the spontaneous form of communitas, which Turner especially advocated, "a congregation or group catches fire in the Spirit." It can also occur in sports or acting explorations, when the players are so spiritually or emotionally connected that they "feel inside the others' heads."[11] Schechner contends that spontaneous communitas does not typically "just happen" but rather needs to be sparked by a ritual act inside of sacred space and time, as was sought in the performative experiments by ensembles like the Living, the Open Theatre, and the Performance Group in this period. For Schechner, "people encounter each other directly, 'nakedly,' in the face-to-face intimate encounter that philosopher Martin Buber called the dialogue of 'I-you' (ich-du)."[12]

The intent of the Living Theatre in the 1960s era, and subsequent evolutions, was indeed to create a sacred space inside the theatrical arena. Active participation in various rites could lead a newly formed community of actors and spectators into a liberated, liminal state where shared, spontaneous communitas might occur. Rite 8 of *Paradise Now* speaks directly to this aim with "The Rite of I and Thou," in which stage directions are as follows: "The actors begin to chant. . . . They begin a rite of the enactment of death. . . . They give a death signal. The signal is the actor's purest statement of his here and now. It is his offering. Between the two moribund beings the holy spark of I and Thou ignites a life force, and . . . they strengthen this contact until the life force between them overcomes the death force . . . and they rise again." As Beck once described the performance, "We wanted to make a play that would no longer be enactment but would be the act itself . . . but always it would be a new experience for us and it would be different from what we called acting." Another key element in creating the possibility of a holy theatre space was an elasticity of time, with many sections of their performance existing in what Viola Spolin once called "the perpetual present,"[13] allowing each individual live encounter to define its own length and shape and the audience to help create the experience. By offering a freewheeling dimension of time and space beyond the borders of the formal proscenium stage, the secular rites of the Living's work in this period allowed for an intimate connection between actor and spectator that could spark liminality, new identities, and a feeling of group communitas. Indeed, longtime members of the company like Tom Walker and Hanon Reznikov first encountered the Living Theatre at these performances as students during the late 1960s, speaking to its enduring, transformative power on some participants.[14]

While the Living Theatre has been distinctive in its commitment to utilizing ritual and audience participation through the present day, numerous other experimental artists of the 1960s probed these boundaries between actor and spectator, life and theatre, and sacred and secular beyond traditional notions of a scripted play in a literal theatre space. Commenting on a similar project (*The Serpent: A Ceremony*, produced by Joe Chaikin and The Open Theatre), collaborator and playwright Jean Claude Van-Itallie recalled that "it was conceived as a piece in which the actors would be priests in a sense; that there would be a feeling of oneness, in the sense the congregation feels the priests are questioning the same kinds of things they are questioning." In the emerging spirit of the times, the Living Theatre and other companies conceived modern-day ceremonial rituals that strove to allow spectators and actors together to explore questions of faith, spirituality, and culture. Traditional drama often supplied answers to dramatic questions, but the deeper intent of the Living Theatre and other like-minded companies was the actual act of participating in the ritual, and seeking the "shape of the questions rather than answers." Exploring the performative act in a live, shared theatre space became a means of seeking individual and collective enlightenment for many radical theatre artists and spectators of this period, with the actors often serving as spiritual guides, secular priests, or shamans of sorts as the ritualistic acts proceeded. As these forms evolved through years of experimentation, spiritual and artistic nourishment was increasingly sought outside of formal performance or any notions of traditional theatre spaces or actor-spectator relationships. This current had a significant impact on the less famous but vital work of the Living Theatre after the 1960s.[15]

Interestingly, despite their unabashed idealism and many reviews dismissing them as naive "hippies," by the end of the 1960s Beck and Malina were actually quite pragmatic in assessing their work as incomplete. Many activists had rejected their message of nonviolent change and spiritual growth, and the company experienced a nagging dissatisfaction with the artifice of "performing" in theatres for mostly middle-class, paying audiences, despite its attempts at converting those theatres into sacred spaces. As former coartistic director Hanon Reznikov noted when the company returned to New York in 2007 from one of many forays abroad, it had experienced numerous changes over six decades but always viewed them as new phases of an ongoing journey. In his words, "The work remains focused on forms that enable the audience to be active participants—not passive spectators."[16] However, the company's focus and approach toward this goal have changed at key junctures, with each phase then informing the next chapter of its work. After publicly breaking their company into four "cells" in 1970 at the height of their fame, Beck and Malina abandoned performing in public theatre spaces throughout the 1970s and early 1980s, concentrating on working directly to improve the conditions of the poor and disenfranchised in prisons and mental hospitals throughout Italy and France, and especially on creating ritualistic acts of street theatre in the slums of Brazil and later in Pittsburgh before returning to Europe in 1975.[17]

While the company eventually found value in again returning to the United States in 1984 to perform in traditional spaces, its international work after 1970 greatly influenced its successive strategies of audience engagement and community building. Despite its abandonment of matrixed theatre spaces, the Living continued to rely on the use of explicitly theatrical techniques in its efforts to connect spiritually to a poor, uneducated, non-Western audience in the favelas, or slum communities, of Brazil. The theoretical underpinning of its work was a further exploration of Beck's interest in the Artaudian notion of pain and "the great scream" as a means of breaking through the numbness and social conditioning of modern industrial life.[18] Once in Brazil, the Living began its work by sending out teams of actors accompanied by Portuguese speakers to meet with the people of Ouro Prêto street by street. Members of the community were interviewed about the nature of their work, dependency on money, and so forth. Integrating themselves into the community and neighborhoods of their intended audience was called "The Campaign" and was continued as an integral part of the Living's interaction in various new (and sometimes initially hostile) communities in subsequent decades. The individual plays of this project, *The Legacy of Cain*, were initially created with local residents of the favelas. *The Mother Day's Play* is representative of this project, involving around 150 students who were asked to write down dreams about their mothers. What emerged from this exploration was a sense of how destructive interpersonal relationships mirrored class tensions in the larger Brazilian socioeconomic system. Another long-term Living Theatre actor, Steven Ben-Israel, noted that most of the parents were poor and black and had typically never been to the theatre before. They encountered their children's dreams through an interactive performance experience based in rituals such as movement, noise, and drumming, with all of them staying afterward for a communal exchange with their children and the Living Theatre performers. Through these projects, the Living initiated a new dialogue about breaking the cycle of spiritual oppression and rampant class inequality plaguing Brazil. Clearly, the nature of these ritualistic, participatory encounters was perceived as empowering and dangerous: the Brazilian government imprisoned the company's actors for several months, eventually forcing them to leave the country.[19]

A look back at this historic journey makes it is clear that the Living's long-standing exploration of alternative social models in various communities, with the hope of achieving a less divisive and spiritually richer life, has led them to return repeatedly to the United States over the years. In my interview with Reznikov in the fall of 2007, he emphasized that he and Malina consciously chose to return to New York after 9/11 and the war on terror abroad. From their perspective, the "focus of so many of the world's problems seemed to be here," creating a new desire to "address these problems with American audiences."[20] However, they initially returned to New York in 1984 to present four new works at the Joyce Theatre. Unfortunately, this was a dark time for the company, as the critics savaged their new repertory and Julian Beck died of cancer in 1985.[21] However, under the coleadership of Malina and Reznikov, the ever-resilient troupe regrouped and embarked on an artistically fertile period with a series of works based out of a new theatre on East Third Street in the Lower East Side of Manhattan. Malina's continuing interest in using ritualistic physical theatre and audience involvement was expressed in interviews from this period:

> My interest is in the unification of the performers and those who have worked on the play with the spectator . . . to find some key to the horrible alienation of people sitting there listening. I think there is something horribly wrong in ignoring one or two hundred people and asking them to sit there quietly and listen to us, the actors. . . . I haven't spent the last twenty years of my

life trying to get the audience to get up and dance and sing in the aisle. Anybody can sing, and dancing is dancing. It's of no interest to me. What I'm talking about is creating for the audience a true role in which choices must be made that will reveal to them their own decision making processes.[22]

Malina also deemed essential the location of the new theatre between Avenues C and D in what was perceived as a poor, dangerous neighborhood: "The Lower East Side has a level of reality. It's got all the horrors, but it also has the poetry of real life, and I think that's where the Living Theatre should be."[23] While this was not a commercially viable choice and the venue always struggled financially before it was closed for code violations in 1993, it did become a vital community center of sorts in a period when homesteaders and squatters clashed frequently with the police around Tompkins Square Park. The Living produced a large body of work there but also offered its space as a meeting place for area artists, activists, and neighbors. As Reznikov remembered, "We created theatrical projects designed to reach out to all these groups. . . . Further, the space became a real point of reference for the struggling community of East Village / Lower East Side artists and activists. All manner of extratheatrical events took place under the Living theatre banner."[24] As in Brazil and Pittsburgh, they engaged issues of concern with local residents through community-based performance. For instance, in the late 1980s, New York officials tried to reclaim empty lots that had been developed as community garden space, which led the Living to create a ritualistic street theatre piece called *Tumult, or Clearing the Streets*. This piece was presented in various public sites around the neighborhood during the summer of 1988, offering support to local residents to preserve community gardens and gather peacefully in public spaces, streets, and parks (and an invitation to participate and express their views).[25]

In addition, the immediate neighborhood had a large homeless problem. The Living opened its doors and collectively created *The Body of God* with members of the homeless population, feeding them daily. As cast member Lois Kagan Mingus recalled, "We talked, as a company, of what we wanted to do in that space. . . . We knew we didn't want to point a finger at it—yes, that's homelessness—or talk about it, or as actors portray it. Let's let the people who are experiencing it now *be* it. That's the way to tell the story."[26] The performance included a section in which the ensemble engaged the audience in small groups about the problem of homelessness and squatters' rights in New York. As with past productions, this created the possibility of a liminal space and encounter, where the "real time" of the performance was suspended to allow for a connection between actors and audiences in the tiny, black box theatre.

I experienced a similar dynamic at the first Living Theatre production I attended at East Third Street, *Tablets*, in 1989. The haunting choral atmosphere of Carlo Altomare's original score effectively melded with the pounding, ritualistic choreography of the highly physical Living Theatre ensemble in a way that captured Artaud's call for a theatre of intoxication and alchemy. As a spectator immersed within the flow of this swirling piece, I viscerally lost touch with "clock time"; the performance climaxed with a silent, embodied encounter between individual actors and spectators in a communal exploration of presence. In that moment, a sense of ritual camaraderie or communitas did seem to fill the space in a way that transcended any need for explanation or articulation: I experienced this in a profound way that is still reverberating with me today.

The Body of God was probably the Living Theatre's most acclaimed work of this period, with critic Roderick Mason Faber calling it a "moving audience participatory work" and "a call to action."[27] However, despite much criticism about their utopianism over the years, Malina and the company were not naive about the play curing the homeless problem in New York. Rather, they were interested in establishing a presence in the community and offering an alternative point of view as they had done in countless past environments. Perhaps most importantly, as area activist and documentary filmmaker Clayton Patterson said, "the Living Theatre showed up,"[28] making an impact despite its relatively short stay on East Third Street.

After another decade or so of working overseas with a home base in Italy, in 1997 the Living Theatre was motivated by a similar rationale to once again return to New York and open a theatre at 21 Clinton Street in the Lower East Side of New York. Reznikov acknowledged the visible gentrification of the area as a change from the 1990s but still felt that the mix of artists, poor people from the old neighborhood, and more recent, upscale residents offered a vital mix and appropriate tension for a new Living Theatre space. Once again, the company envisioned the theatre not just as a site to perform plays but also as a gathering place that could energize a new community of artists, activists, and audience members interested in social equality and justice. After a successful revival of their early off-Broadway play *The Brig*, their first new collective creation was a large cast piece entitled *Eureka*. Sadly, Reznikov died unexpectedly in May 2008; Malina completed the finished version by October of that year. Inspired by Edgar Allan Poe's treatise on the nature of the universe, Reznikov saw the structure of the play as "allowing the audience to feel as if they are creating the universe as a metaphor for their own lives."[29] The *New York Times* questioned the ideology and intention of *Eureka* as follows:

The unflappably earnest performers direct the audience members' actions by whispers and by example. . . . Sometimes it's difficult to interpret and sometimes silly, as self-consciousness and embarrassment threaten to take over. . . . And certain questions linger. Can the audience-performer divide be broken down without establishing a new hierarchy of leaders (the performers) and followers? (A small coalition of the unwilling slunk off to the sidelines.) How do we think about the theatrical experience when we're participants? But a clear point floats above the physical action: "You are the answer," someone says. If creation is continuous, and we're part of it, we can change things. This is where Ms. Malina's heart seems to lie, even if the show's politics . . . can seem diffuse and unfocused.[30]

The review certainly encapsulates the tension surrounding the obstacle of generating a transcendent, genuine level of audience involvement, something company members have wrestled with since the 1960s, when, as Reznikov once wryly noted, they "were the mainstream culture's favorite flavor of the month."[31] When the Living Theatre returned to the United States in 1984, critics charged that it was out of touch with the postmodern experimental and conservative cultural currents of that period. The company endured a series of negative and even antagonistic reviews through the 1990s, although since returning in 2007 it has generally been treated favorably in the New York press as a venerable and historically important institution. Individual productions can still come under attack in a way that seems uniquely linked to the company's ideology and radical past, as when *Village Voice* reviewer Jacob Gallagher-Ross entitled his review of *Korach* in 2010 "The Living Theatre Inflicts *Korach* on Local Ticket Holders" and said, "No one seems to have told the Living Theatre the '60s are over."[32]

I find this sort of comment quite reductive in responding to the work of the Living, as its members themselves have repeatedly acknowledged cultural and audience shifts over the decades, using their forms today to generate new ideas and work with young people around the globe. Furthermore, unlike most traditional companies, the Living Theatre has never been driven by a desire for profits or good reviews. As Malina and Reznikov noted in a 2004 letter to supporters, "We have always wanted to work, not necessarily where we are most popular, but rather where we are most needed."[33] Positive or negative reviews aside, Malina and the company are well aware of the challenge of generating an authentic level of noncoerced audience participation with their productions. Having seen most of their work during the late 1980s and 1990s, I agree that despite the Living's best intentions and efforts, some audiences often seemed reluctant to engage it directly and seek communitas. (An exception to this was its production of *Utopia* in 1996.) The more generous review of *Ko-*

rach in the *Times* spoke to this problem when critic Eric Grode observed, "This being the Living Theater, the audience-performer divide blurs at the end, as cast members cajole one and all into standing, dancing, joining hands and vocalizing with them. . . . At the performance I attended, however, one lone audience member refused to join in, hunching defiantly in her seat . . . the battle continues."[34]

For me, the image of a sole audience member seated with symbolic "arms crossed" in defiant opposition represents the crux of the Living's ongoing mission. As discussed throughout this essay, the company has deliberately chosen a path innately filled with tensions and obstacles, in service of an openly optimistic, spiritual goal beyond the materialism of capitalist, corporate culture. As Malina proclaimed in her director's notes for *Utopia*, "If we are not yet ready to create utopia, we can at least enact it. . . . Our intention in working on a play about utopia is to overcome the spectator's disbelief in her own desires."[35] Despite its seemingly unshakable belief in the possibility of utopia, the company has always been willing to confront real-life poverty and oppression, often outside the safe confines of a theatre space, from the slums of Brazil and New York to the war-torn zones of Lebanon. In a 2002 interview in New York, Reznikov discussed their work with forty students in Lebanon on the site of a former prison that had been converted to a "museum of torture" by the Hezbollah regime. Once again, the Living utilized its theatrical forms to encourage students to explore the possibilities of nonviolent response to their violence-ridden present reality. Both Reznikov and Malina spoke to the importance of using the theatrical encounter to communicate a message of hope in the face of an undeniably difficult, frightening situation, to "take all the hopeful energy and optimism that is available now and flame it, fan it, and act it out in the streets."[36] Of course, that collective aim extends to any "defiant" audience members sitting in the safer confines of the Clinton Street theatre as well.

While Malina and the company are focused on making theatre that is valid in our historical and cultural moment, they continue to use many of their forms and techniques generated over the decades to connect with young students and new audiences. Malina and Brad Burgess, the company's managing director and Malina's assistant on several productions, have discussed their idiosyncratic approach to casting and rehearsal as emblematic of their quest for a "better" way of allowing human behavior to flourish. The Living Theatre rarely auditions actors, believing that people who need to work with them will find a way. As Burgess puts it, "The people who belong to us come to us and we welcome them."[37] In rehearsals, every company member contributes ideas. Unlike in traditional theatre rehearsals, actors give other actors feedback at times. While this can create tension in the moment, the company believes this is offset by the ultimate creation of a model of consensus and authentic expression that values the creative and personal contribution of each cast member. The Living has always welcomed newcomers who work in tandem with veteran performers, some of whom first performed with the Living Theatre in the late 1960s and early 1970s. For a young artist like Burgess, who joined the company only several years ago, "having these people here, it's like a choreography that comes from the Living Theatre technique that they're passing on to a lot of the new folks."[38] This process has been extended outside the formal bounds of the company's rehearsal process through workshops in the Living Theatre technique that members of the company share on college campuses across the United States as well as overseas (Living Theatre Europa). These workshops reflect Malina's self-description as a "missionary,"[39] providing tools to the students that allow them to express their voice, desires, and visions for the future in a realized public performance, including street theatre. The Living Theatre workshop leaders are interested in posing questions that the students must begin to answer in their collective efforts to create a new, authentic community and possible new identities as global citizens.

Jerry Goralnick, a veteran actor who started working with the company at East Third Street, often conducts workshops on college campuses with other Living Theatre members such as Lois Kagan Mingus and Tom Walker. Goralnick spoke to the power of ritual in the company's forms and the impact of this work on the spirituality of many young workshop participants:

> There is an immediacy to the ritual form that is attractive to young people. If we accept the idea that we are born rational beings into an absurd world we can easily see why young minds confronting this need a powerful release. This is one reason why music and dancing are so important. The nervous system needs pathways to deal with this disconnect. As we get older we can more appreciate the subtleties and intricacies of theatrical literature in addressing primal questions of existence. When we are young we just want to jump and shout because that is an immediate way to deal with the oppression of a system that we are born into. All through our history momentous occasions; birth, death, puberty and marriage have had rituals created to allow the psyche to process these passages. In our workshops we introduce the students to techniques for giving voice to their most elemental feelings. To find the truth in a theatrical character and then to bring your own truth to creating that character for the stage you have to first have an understanding of who you are. Ritual forms are the key to these discoveries. The Living

Theatre's deeply founded belief in pacifism and anarchism as a way to exist in society offers a sensible solid cosmology for a young person just beginning to find their way in the world. It's a moral bedrock from which the person can then diverge. The exercises we use in our creative process that have·been developed from the work of Artaud, the surrealists and the anarchists provide insight to the young actor about themselves and their place in the world and provide building blocks that can then be used in addressing characters and texts in the theatrical canon.[40]

This unique mix of artists sharing an embodied history of the company's technique is clearly focused on engaging new audiences in the present, but working within the legacy and spirit of the 1960s era experiments that sought transcendence through theatrical encounter rather than traditional religious ceremonies. Malina believes that the "ensemble is the only useful form of theatre. . . . You don't see that much any more. An actor gets a job . . . goes to another company, etc. We want to develop a company . . . from one play to another from one year to another." Thus, the Living seeks to develop the same sense of community and spiritual empowerment at home, within its ensemble, which is then extended to its audiences. Malina feels its approach to theatre is still important "because of the participatory role that the audience plays in the play." Its mission can be achieved only when the audience actively helps with the development of the play, too; Malina notes that a core audience keeps coming back and "teaching" company members as well in a spiritually reciprocal relationship.[41]

All of these currents seem to have collided in the Living's production in January 2012 of the ambitiously titled *History of the World*. The *New York Times* noted its sprawling, episodic structure: "With helpful actor guides, we rocket from prehistory . . . the French Revolution; the Industrial Revolution; the Internet; and, of course, Occupy Wall Street."[42] Questions are asked such as "Where were you at the death of Gandhi?" prompting the audience to examine themselves and their value systems as is customary with the Living Theatre. Perhaps more than any other recent work in the company's repertory, *History of the World* requires the audience to participate in the production's ritual and create the reality that they desire. The theatre's seats have been removed and the action of the play constantly moves across the space, with actors often intermingling with the spectators as the audience is continually guided to stand, travel, and participate. The evening culminates with a ritualistic scene set amidst Greek gods: several cast members disrobe, leaving themselves vulnerable and exposed as they begin a choral chant that segues to song. As the scene evolves, ideally the audience becomes one with the cast in a group communitas involving shared touch, song, and sacred space, blurring any and all matrixed, formal lines between actors and spectators in the intimate, potentially liminal space of the Clinton Street theatre.[43]

Two reviews regarding the level of audience response at the play's end are interesting to consider. Andy Webster of the *Times* described the audience in a circle chanting, with Malina seated on a chair exhorting the "nonviolent anarchist revolution to come." Webster observed Malina interacting with the "20 odd cast members" and spectator-performers after the formal production had ceased: "This aging lioness lets out a considerable roar."[44] Mitch Montgomery of *Back Stage* referred to Malina as a legendary artist but offered a mixed perspective on the play's ending: "Malina . . . is well-intentioned in trying to cultivate a new crop of artistic revolutionaries, but by the time she begins intoning from the sidelines . . . the experience takes on an unsettling, almost cultish swerve." Montgomery does temper his review by commenting, "Each viewing of *History of the World* will certainly be different due to the interactive components. It's worth noting that everyone else at the performance I attended was fully absorbed and thrilled by the experience."[45]

Montgomery's description of the audience mirrors the enthusiasm of the audience participation I observed in several recorded performance clips. That fervor contrasts markedly to my memory of the Living's revival of *Mysteries and Smaller Pieces* in 1997, when I was struck by the lack of audience participation in the company's historic "chord" exercise (where actors and spectators form a circle with arms around each other and intone a choral sound with the goal of achieving a unified sense of group expression). As was discussed earlier, many ecstatic spectators of the 1960s radical theatre sought a spiritual connection through the secular rituals of the live theatre space. In the context of a recently more energized and radicalized youth culture stemming in part from the Occupy Wall Street movement, the Living's style of ritualistic, participatory theatre is perhaps once again in sync with an emerging, still-growing contemporary zeitgeist. Its dominant audience seemed eager to have an opportunity to seek a liminal, transformative experience through the theatrical encounter of *History of the World*, allowing them to transcend temporarily the current social and economic turmoil outside the cocoon of the theatre space.

Still, as in the past, what most interests Malina and the Living Theatre is how that spiritual experience might ripple beyond the limited duration of the play into the spectator's daily life, creating long-term changes in identity and social systems as happens in an authentic liminal experience. For Malina, the answers are found in "education through art—that's our part of the work, to make clear we don't need punishment, prisons, etc. There are other ways to deal with our social problems or how to get along with each other" and make the world a better place.[46] "I think we have to think in a very broad vision of the possibility of another kind of life. And move towards it even though we're not there."[47] The Living Theatre of today still engages vital social issues of material and spiritual blight, continuing to utilize ritual in performance as a tool to allow spectators to envision and hopefully embody their better, transformed selves and an ideal utopian community. The ongoing goal of the Living to nourish each individual spectator's spiritual life, often amid harsh economic or sociopolitical circumstances, has carried over from its fervent years of experimentation in the 1960s. The many challenges over the decades, however, have also added a level of pragmatism, with Malina contending in an interview shortly after Reznikov's death, "Our mission is to redeem our lousy, violent world insofar as we can. If we take a half-inch step, we take a half-inch step . . . it depends on what we can do at that time."[48]

The viscerally charged audience response to *History of the World* indicates such a possible step forward for the community of spectators and actors who shared the collective encounter of that particular live, ritualistic experience. As Tom F. Driver observed in his work *Liberating Rites*, "Human longing for ritual is deep, and in our culture often frustrated. . . . The ability of rituals to assist in the transformation of society, which I have called part of their magic, is not magic in a fantastical sense. . . . Agents of transformation, rituals are themselves transformed by the histories to which they belong."[49] The long-standing spiritual mission of Malina, Beck, and Reznikov's Living Theatre remains challenging, ongoing, and at times intoxicating, working to create the vision of a theatre as a holy place where transformational ritual can happen. Shortly after opening the theatre at 21 Clinton Street, Reznikov expressed a desire that "perhaps we'll be able to pass on the torch here . . . and searching young spirits of future generations will come to know our particular blend of art and zeal first-hand."[50] At the time of this writing, Malina and her company have launched an appeal to supporters to raise $24,000 within two weeks to avoid eviction from their theatre. While the Living Theatre hopes to establish a stable financial lease within the next five years in New York, its long journey traversing numerous spiritual and material homes reflects its own continual transformation as its members engage "the history to which they belong." As Reznikov proclaimed shortly before his death, "The essential goal at Third Street was the goal we are pursuing now— to create a space suited to that particular encounter of actor, audience, and the idea of freedom that we call The Living."[51]

Notes

1. Julian Beck, quoted in *Uptown Dispatch*, October 1985. "Living Theatre Collection," Papers 1945–Present, Series 13, Boxes 43–47, Billy Rose Theatre Collection, Lincoln Center, New York City.

2. Julian Beck, quoted in *Signals through the Flames*, directed by Sheldon Rochlin (Mystic Fire Video, 1983), videocassette.

3. Margaret Croyden, *Lunatics, Lovers and Poets: The Contemporary Experimental Theatre* (New York: McGraw-Hill, 1974), 62, 63; Christopher Innes, *Avant Garde Theatre* (New York: Routledge, 1993), 174.

4. Victor Turner, *The Ritual Process: Structure and Anti-Structure* (Chicago: Aldine Publishing, 1969), 95.

5. Richard Schechner, *Performance Studies*, 2nd ed. (New York: Routledge, 2006), 66, 67.

6. Ibid.

7. Ibid.

8. Judith Malina, quoted in "Judith Malina and The Living Theatre's Production of Korach," interview on "Let Them Talk–Live," New York, YouTube video, 27:58, posted January 27, 2011, http://www.youtube.com/watch?v=0Cjmfqk73z4&playnext=1&list=PLC532CAF5F9EBB0A5&feature=results_video.

9. Saul Gottlieb, "The Living Theatre in Exile," *Tulane Drama Review* 10 (Summer 1966): 140–45; Pierre Biner, *The Living Theatre*, trans. Robert Meister (New York, Avon Books, 1972).

10. Patrick McDermott, "Portrait of an Actor, Watching," *TDR* 13 (Spring 1969): 80.

11. Turner, *Drama, Fields and Metaphors* (Ithaca, NY: Cornell University Press, 1974), 274; Schechner, *Performance Studies*, 70–71.

12. Schechner, "Containment Is the Enemy: Judith Malina and Julian Beck interviewed by Richard Schechner," *TDR* 13 (Spring 1969): 25–26.

13. Viola Spolin, interviewed in *Flashing on the Sixties*, directed by Lisa Law (Pyramid Film, 1991), DVD.

14. "Collective Creation of The Living Theatre," written down by Judith Malina and Julian Beck, *Paradise Now* (New York: Vintage Books, 1971), 135; Schechner, "Containment Is the Enemy," 25.

15. The Open Theatre, "'*The Serpent*,' Part 1: A Brief Documentary," interview with Jean Claude Van-Itallie, YouTube video, 8:52, posted April 29, 2010, http://www.youtube.com/watch?v=FB2OHclka5o; Michael Kirby, "The New Theatre," *The Tulane Drama Review* 10, no. 2 (Winter 1965): 25–26.

16. Hanon Reznikov, New York, phone interview with the author, September 2007.

17. Erika Munk, "Paradise Later: An Interview with Judith Malina and Julian Beck," *Performance* 1 (December 1971): 91–97.

18. Beck, quoted in *Signals through the Flames*.

19. Paul Ryder Ryan, "The Living Theatre in Brazil," *TDR* (Summer 1971):

23–24; John Tytell, *The Living Theatre: Art, Exile, and Outrage* (New York: Grove Press, 1995), 289–304; Arthur Sanier, *The New Radical Theatre Notebook* (New York: Applause Books, 1997), 250–55.

20. Reznikov, interview with the author, 2007.

21. Arthur Sanier, "The Several Embattled Stages of The Living Theatre," *Theater* 16, no. 2 (Spring 1985): 52–57.

22. Malina, quoted in Renfreu Neff, "Judith Malina: Living Tradition, Living Theater," *Theater Week*, January 25–31, 1988, 26.

23. Ibid., 27.

24. Reznikov, quoted in Cindy Rosenthal, *Hanon Reznikov: Living on Third Street: Plays of the Living Theatre, 1989–1992* (New York: Autonomedia Press, 2008), 29.

25. Rosenthal, *Hanon Reznikov*, 15–16.

26. Kagan Mingus, quoted in Rosenthal, *Hanon Reznikov*, 17.

27. Faber, quoted in Rosenthal, *Hanon Reznikov*, 17.

28. Patterson, quoted in Rosenthal, *Hanon Reznikov*, 17–18.

29. Reznikov, interview with the author, 2007.

30. Rachel Saltz, theatre review of *Eureka*, performed by The Living Theatre, New York, "Audience Participation, Poe, and Politics in a Big Bang," *New York Times*, October 8, 2008, http://theater.nytimes.com/2008/10/08/theater/reviews/08eure.html?_r=.

31. Reznikov quoted in Rosenthal, *Hanon Reznikov*, 30.

32. Jacob Gallagher-Ross, review of *Korach* performed by The Living Theatre, New York, December 15, 2010, "The Living Theatre Inflicts *Korach* on Local Ticket Holders," *Village Voice*, http://www.villagevoice.com/2010-12-15/theater/the-living-theatre-inflicts-korach-on-local-ticket-holders.

33. Malina and Reznikov, "Dear Friends Letter," 1989 ("Living Theatre Collection," New York).

34. Eric Grode, "A Man So Stubborn He Wouldn't Even Listen to Moses," review of *Korach*, performed by The Living Theatre, New York, *New York Times*, December 21, 2010, http://theater.nytimes.com/2010/12/22/theater/reviews/22korach.html?_r=.

35. Malina, program notes, *Utopia*, performed by The Living Theatre, New York (personal collection of the author).

36. "Conversations with Harold Hudson Channer," interview with Judith Malina and Hanon Reznikov, New York, YouTube video, 58:04, air date March 3, 2002, posted by Harold Hudson Channer, May 13, 2008, http://www.youtube.com/watch?v=exp9bmBReFo.

37. Burgess, quoted in "Let Them Talk–Live" interview, 2011, http://www.youtube.com/watch?v=oCjmfqk73z4&playnext=1&list=PLC532CAF5F9EBB0A5&feature=results_videohttp.

38. Ibid.

39. Malina, quoted in "Gerald Thomas Interviews Judith Malina," New York, YouTube video, 7:31, uploaded October 7, 2008, http://www.youtube.com/watch?v=HY9CBK_oDTQ.

40. Jerry Goralnick, e-mail interview with the author, April 2012.

41. Malina, quoted in "Let Them Talk–Live" interview, 2011, http://www.youtube.com/watch?v=oCjmfqk73z4&playnext=1&list=PLC532CAF5F9EBB0A5&feature=results_video.

42. Andy Webster, "From the Crucifixion to the Internet, You Are There," review of *History of the World*, performed by The Living Theatre, New York, *New York Times*, http://theater.nytimes.com/2012/01/25/theater/reviews/history-of-the-world-at-the-living-theater.html.

43. The Living Theatre, *History of the World*, recorded live on ustream, YouTube video, 14:15, January 1, 2012, http://www.youtube.com/watch?v=aiFBTBFsZwg; The Living Theatre, *History of the World*, LRS.FM-Radio/TV, YouTube video, 13:21, January 1, 2012, 2:09 A.M., http://www.youtube.com/watch?v=o2iiw3FnKiQ; The Living Theatre, *History of the World*, LRS.FM-Radio/TV-hmmm, YouTube video, 9:12, January 1, 2012, http://www.youtube.com/watch?v=XmjPxFEszs8http.

44. Webster, "From the Crucifixion to the Internet, You Are There."

45. Mitch Montgomery, "*History of the World* at the Living Theater," review of *History of the World*, performed by The Living Theatre, New York, January 13, 2012, Backstaqe, http://www.backstage.com/review/ny-theater/off-off-broadway/history-of-the-world.

46. Malina, quoted in "Let Them Talk–Live" interview, 2011, http://www.youtube.com/watch?v=oCjmfqk73z4&playnext=1&list=PLC532CAF5F9EBB0A5&feature=results_video.

47. Malina, quoted in Channer interview, 2002, http://www.youtube.com/watch?v=exp9bmBReF.

48. Malina, quoted in "Gerald Thomas Interview," 2011, http://www.youtube.com/watch?v=HY9CBK_oDTQhttp.

49. Tom F. Driver, *Liberating Rites: Understanding the Transformative Power of Ritual* (BookSurge, 2006), 184.

50. Reznikov, quoted in Rosenthal, *Hanon Reznikov*, 193.

51. Ibid.

Top Brass

Theatricality, Themes, and Theology in James Weldon Johnson's *God's Trombones*

Gregory S. Carr

T HE HARLEM Renaissance gave America some of its most gifted writers. Zora Neale Hurston regaled her readers with her many tales of Eatonville, Florida, while her sometime friend Langston Hughes painted life in Harlem with broad strokes of both humor and anger. Another literary giant of the Harlem Renaissance, James Weldon Johnson, contributed (among many other significant works) a collection of seven prose sermons and an opening prayer written in the style of the liturgies of the traditional black church. *God's Trombones* remains one of the great treasures of the Harlem Renaissance and of American poetry. Although written as literature, *God's Trombones* is inherently theatrical. The poems' rich language illustrates many contextual themes present within the traditional black church worship experience, humanizes the often-caricatured black preacher, and is readily adaptable for the theatre.

Theatrical adaptations of *God's Trombones* have been staged regularly since its publication in 1927. In 1952, *God's Trombones* was featured on popular bandleader Fred Waring's television variety show. This production marked the first time an African American appeared on the program. Frank Davis portrayed one of the preachers and also sang Negro spirituals with the Waring Glee Club.[1] In 1963, actress Vinnette Carroll adapted Johnson's work into the gospel musical *Trumpets of the Lord*. The musical, produced off-Broadway that year at the Astor Place Playhouse, enjoyed a run of 160 performances.[2] A revival of this production was staged in 1969 by Theodore Mann, one of the original producers. The revival ran for one week at Mann's Circle in the Square.[3] *Trumpets of the Lord* was remounted in New York by producer Woodie King in 1988 at the Shubert Theatre and in 1989 at the New Federal Theatre and at the Theatre of Riverside Church.[4] Most recently, Johnson's masterpiece has received a revival of sorts at the Karamu Theatre in Cleveland, Ohio. Karamu artistic director Terrence Spivey has successfully staged an adaptation of *God's Trombones* for three consecutive years. The Karamu productions have featured an ensemble of preachers, singers, and dancers from the Cleveland community. *Cleveland Plain Dealer* columnist Chuck Yarborough praised the recent production for its energy and creativity and a cast "which ranges from graybeards to junior-high kids."[5]

Among the contextual themes vividly illustrated by *God's Trombones* is the celebration of the call-and-response ritual of the traditional black church. Kenyon College's "North by South," a three-year study of African American migrations from South to North sponsored by the National Endowment for the Humanities, describes this "alternation between leader and chorus, often called call-and-response" as a "defining . . . [and] important element of African American music."[6] Call-and-response has its roots in the ceremonial songs of West African villages. These chants traveled across the Atlantic Ocean in the bowels of slave ships during the Middle Passage as a means of communication and landed in the cotton fields of the South in the form of work songs and "field hollers." From there, they grew into Negro spirituals and the gospel hymnody of the black church.[7]

The call-and-response phenomenon intrinsic to *God's Trombones* is vividly portrayed in the sermon "Go Down Death—a Funeral Sermon." In the Karamu Theatre's 2012 production, actor Kenny Charles skillfully used his formidable voice to elicit responses from both the cast and the audience. Spectator and performer alike encouraged Sister Caroline to transition from death to the heavenly gates of glory:

> Weep not—weep not.
> She is not dead
> She's resting in the bosom of Jesus.[8]

Another contextual characteristic inherent to traditional black worship and woven into *God's Trombones* is the music. Dramatizations of the piece have been colored with the melodies of hymns, spirituals, and even gospel music. *God's Trombones* successfully integrates these musical genres both to complement Johnson's prose and to advance the narrative. While Vinnette Carroll's adaptation, *Trumpets of the Lord*, integrated new songs into the production, the classic Negro spiritual "Were You There?" was also a part of the musical repertoire. The sermon "The Crucifixion" is often augmented by the poignant lyrics of "Were You There?":

> Were you there when they crucified my Lord?
> Were you there when they crucified my Lord?

Oh! Sometimes it causes me to tremble, tremble, tremble.
Were you there when they crucified my Lord?[9]

A figure of note in *God's Trombones* is the preacher—the sermonizer.
In "Art, Literature, and the Harlem Renaissance: The Messages of *God's
Trombones*," Anne Carroll relates Johnson's thoughts about the black
preacher: "He [Johnson] recalls hearing the sermons as a boy, and . . .
recounts an incident in his adulthood. While traveling on a speaking cir-
cuit, Johnson had been taken to a church late in the evening, where he
had witnessed a stunning performance by a visiting preacher. Johnson
found himself fascinated—and as he writes, he was, 'perhaps against my
will, deeply moved.'"[10] Johnson himself said that "the old-time Negro
preacher has not yet been given the niche in which he properly belongs."[11]

Too often, black preachers had been caricatured through the overuse
of Negro dialect or the blatant stereotyping typical of that era (and not
unknown in our own). Michael North, commenting on Johnson's realistic and sensitive treatment, compares it to an early dramatic sketch by
T. S. Eliot intended to be performed in the minstrel tradition that included the character "Rev. Hammond Aigs, comic negro minister, of the
'come breddern' type." North argues that Johnson departs from the traditional rhyme and Negro dialect of predecessors such as Eliot and Paul
Laurence Dunbar and embraces the modern prose of Walt Whitman. Carl
Van Vechten, a white patron of many Harlem Renaissance artists, claims
that Johnson's "The Creation" was the poem that "broke the chain of
dialect which bound [them] . . . and freed the younger generation from
this dangerous restraint."[12]

It is in this context that we see how Johnson frees the black preacher
from the manacles of minstrelsy and liberates him into a three-dimensional
reality. For instance, in "Let My People Go," the preacher speaks not only
of the biblical Pharaoh of Egypt, but of the Jim Crow system of segre-
gation that denied him and his people their citizenship. Johnson elabo-
rates: "What the colored poet in the United States needs to do is something like what Synge did for the Irish; he needs to find a form that will
express the racial spirit by symbols from within rather than symbols from
without, such as the mere mutilation of English spelling and pronuncia-
tion. He needs a form that is freer and larger than dialect form express-
ing the imagery, the idioms, the peculiar terms of thought and distinctive humor and pathos, too, of the Negro."[13]

Recognizing the role of the preacher as master storyteller is the key to
understanding the cultural context of the black church itself. The black
preacher calls upon his or her "sanctified imagination" or creative license
to anthropomorphize God. Johnson describes God as a tender "Mammy

bending over her baby"[14] or as an upright judge at a cosmological court date offering heaven to the righteous and eternal damnation to the sinners. The preacher employs the "whoop," a musical, singsong delivery; this mode of delivery invites the congregation to participate in the worship service and encourages an ecstatic release or catharsis through dancing, shouting, and the playing of the tambourine or drums, enabling the sermon to be preached with "Holy Ghost" power. The preacher may call, "Can I get a witness?" to which the congregation might enthusiastically respond by saying, "Go 'head preacher, go 'head now!" At the emotional peak of his sermon, the preacher might be spontaneously joined by the church organist, who, upon "feeling the spirit," might joyfully play a musical scale in incremental half steps, complementing the preacher with each melodic phrase coupled with swelling arpeggios. The preacher's goal is to reach a fever pitch that ends in a spiritual denouement for all, thus signaling the "opening of the doors of the church" for some poor sinner, backslider, or wayward saint to give his or her life over (or back) to the Lord.

Trazana Beverley, a Tony award–winning actress, portrayed a preacher in Woodie King's 1989 production. She observes the double standard applied to women preachers in the polity of the black church:

> Female preachers have always had a hard way to go. In our discussion, Woodie was citing some female preachers from the period of the Wild West who were not allowed to have a church, who were subsequently compelled to move from town to town. And I have seen pictures of these ladies who have their robes and their Bibles. It's a wonderful thing to look at, and you realize nothing's changed. Nothing's new. Such a woman could not be a wimp or a weakling to go out on the road by herself, or maybe with one companion. She might have ridden a buckboard or a horse and carried a gun. She might have been married with children but felt this was something she had to do. So she was out on the road for so many days a month preaching. Being a Black woman, she was probably ostracized by the towns she went into.[15]

God's Trombones is a highly adaptable piece of classic literature that mirrors the cultural norms of the traditional black church worship service; employs call-and-response and sacred songs to exemplify the musical and communal aspects of the black church; explores the theme of black liberation; and elevates the black preacher. When Johnson's words are spoken aloud and his poems theatricalized, the power of his language is released like mighty music. Commenting of the title of his piece, Johnson summarizes by describing a black preacher in full swing. He compares the voice of the preacher to an instrument "possessing above all others the power to express the wide and varied range of emotions encompassed by the human voice. . . . He strode the pulpit up and down in what was actually a very rhythmic dance, and he brought into play the full gamut of his wonderful voice, a voice—what shall I say?—not of an organ or a trumpet, but rather of a trombone."[16]

Notes

1. "First DVD from Fred Waring's America to Premiere," *Penn State Live* (January 2009), http://live.psu.edu/story/37225.

2. Thomas Hischak, *Off-Broadway Musicals since 1919: From Greenwich Follies to the Toxic Avenger* (New York: Scarecrow Press, 2011).

3. Ibid., 86.

4. Bernard L. Peterson, *A Century of Musicals in Black and White: An Encyclopedia of Musical Stage Works by, about, or Involving African Americans* (Westport, CT: Greenwood Press, 1993), 148.

5. Chuck Yarborough, "*God's Trombones'* Testify to the Power of Sermons, Verse and Choreography in Karamu House Performance" *Cleveland Plain Dealer*, March 22, 2012, http://www.cleveland.com/arts/index.ssf/2012/03/gods_trombones_testify_to_the.html.

6. "The Influence of Africa: Syncopation, Call and Response, and Timbre," North by South, Kenyon College, http://northbysouth.kenyon.edu/1998/music/rhythm/rhythm.htm.

7. Cain Hope Felder, *Stony the Road We Trod: African American Biblical Interpretation* (Minneapolis: Fortress Press), 103.

8. James Weldon Johnson, *God's Trombones: Seven Negro Sermons in Verse* (New York: Viking Press, 1927), 30.

9. Traditional lyrics.

10. Anne Carroll, "Art, Literature, and the Harlem Renaissance: The Messages of *God's Trombones*," *College Literature* 29, no. 3 (2002): 57.

11. Johnson, *God's Trombones*, 2.

12. Cited in Michael North, *The Dialect of Modernism: Race, Language, and Twentieth-Century Literature* (New York: Oxford University Press, 1994), 10.

13. Ibid., 57.

14. Johnson, *God's Trombones*, 20.

15. Michael S. Weaver, "Women of Belief: Black Church and Black Theatre: An Interview with Trazana Beverley." *Black American Literature Form* 25, no. 1 (1991), 121.

16. Quoted in North, *Dialect of Modernism*, 10.

Pretty's Got Me All Bent Out of Shape

Jordan Harrison's *Act a Lady* and
the Ritual of Queerness

Matt DiCintio

I N ROBERT ANDERSON'S *Tea and Sympathy* (1953), Laura Reynolds delivers what passes as a revelation to young Tom Lee before she locks the door, unbuttons her blouse, and requests that years from now, he speak of the ensuing encounter kindly: "Manliness is not all swagger and swearing and mountain climbing. Manliness is also tenderness, gentleness, consideration. You men think you can decide on who is a man, when only a woman can really know."[1] A half century after the lights dimmed with Tom's hand at Laura's breast, Jordan Harrison's *Act a Lady*, which premiered at the Humana Festival in 2006, exemplifies what has become possible for young men in queer theatre. Harrison is using the American stage to dismantle hegemonic assumptions about gender roles and sexual relevancy, as opposed to Anderson and his contemporaries, who perpetuated what Eve Sedgwick has called a "crisis of homo/heterosexual definition."[2]

Act a Lady is a response to John M. Clum's "challenge for post-*Boys in the Band* and post-Stonewall gay dramatists to find forms more suited to the creation of a positive gay self."[3] Clum has observed that "in traditional, realistic drama, there is no meaningful place for gay experiences or explorations and expressions of what has been inadequately called the 'gay sensibility.'"[4] Still, as Victor Turner writes in *From Ritual to Theatre*, "Theatre in complex, urbanized societies on the scale of 'civilizations' has become a specialized domain, where it has become legitimate to experiment with modes of presentation, many of which radically (and indeed, consciously) depart from Aristotle's model."[5] With that specialization, we can see how Harrison is kinder to his gay boy than Anderson was to his straight boy. Turner continues: "Through the performance it-self, what is normally sealed up, inaccessible to everyday observation and reasoning, in the depth of sociocultural life, is drawn forth—[Wilhelm] Dilthey uses the term *Ausdruck*, 'an expression,' from *ausdrucken*, lit-erally, 'to press or squeeze out.'"[6] To paraphrase the hypermasculine, moonshine-swilling bad boy True in *Act a Lady*, pretty's got Harrison's characters all bent out of shape. They do not need to return to the sta-tus quo ante of Tom's hand and Laura's breast.[7]

In demonstrating how queerness in *Act a Lady* manifests as ritual-istic, I recall the distinction Victor Turner has made between the "tribal-liminal" and the "industrial-liminoid,"[8] particularly his assessment that the liminal in tribal societies cannot be subversive, but the liminoid in postagrarian industrial societies can be.[9] Still, concluding his 1977 essay "Variations on a Theme of Liminality," Turner notes, "It remains true that in complex societies today's liminoid is yesterday's liminal."[10]

In "Reclaiming the Discourse of Camp," Moe Meyer argues that "what 'queer' signals is an ontological challenge that displaces bourgeois notions of the Self as unique, abiding, and continuous while substituting instead a concept of the Self as performative, improvisational, discontinu-ous, and processually constituted by repetitive and stylized acts."[11] I sug-gest that Meyer's "ontological challenge" constitutes the queer ritual in *Act a Lady* and ultimately answers John Clum's call for a suitable form. Such a ritual may be "today's liminoid," but because the self-actualization of the young gay man, Casper, requires him to undergo the "ontological challenge," the play indeed constitutes a "social drama."

In "The Queer Root of Theater," Laurence Senelick writes that "queer theater has an advantage in that its most essential component, sexual un-orthodoxy, still packs a considerable punch, for all the commercialization of the gay image . . . the enactment of sexual scenarios and gender meta-morphosis still aims for the viscera."[12] In *Act a Lady*, that aim is also to legitimize. According to Eli Rozik, "Although secular rituals do not share the intention to reach the sacred, they may equally well fulfill these sec-ondary functions [of promoting a sense of community and social cohe-sion, and bestowing legitimation of social and political order]."[13]

With my investigation of Harrison's play, I do not mean to suggest that Turner's (or anyone's) model of liminality may be arbitrarily ap-plied merely because only the liminoid is available to modern society. I do suggest that queerness in *Act a Lady* serves a "subculture," defined by Dick Hebdige as "the expressive forms and rituals of those subordinate groups . . . who are alternately dismissed, denounced and canonized; treated at different times as threats to public order and as harmless buffoons."[14] Although Hebdige's focus is the conflict among generations and classes, his conclusion that subcultures "do not stand outside the reflexive circuitry of production and reproduction which links together, at least on a symbolic level, the separate and fragmented pieces of the social totality"[15] is applicable to how the treatment of gay men has evolved in the past half century. To understand *Act a Lady* as such a subculture allows us to chart the evolution of challenges to heteronormativity. The challenges that were once eliminated by ideology (Tom is not gay, and Mr. Harris, the teacher who is dismissed for bathing nude with Tom, never appears onstage) come out in *Act a Lady* (Casper is gay, and pretty bends all the men out of shape).

A synopsis of the play: In 1927, the Elks Club of Wattleburg, a small Midwestern town, is producing a faux canonical play from Revolution-era France, and men of the town are cast as the play's leading ladies. In their play, Lady Romola and Countess Roquefort each hope for a proposal from Vicomte Valentino Ufa, but the maid Greta is his true love. After Roquefort causes the fatal crash of Romola's carriage, Greta steals the Lady's emerald and flees to Liechtenstein disguised as a man. While Greta and Ufa rendezvous on the Ile St. Louis, Lady Romola's ghost returns to haunt them all and reclaim her jewel. The Elks Club rehearsals culminate in a nearly catastrophic but ultimately successful performance for the town.

The plot of *Act a Lady* mirrors the processual form Turner has described across several works as a breach that introduces liminality before reintegration.[16] In the play's first scene, we see the status quo. Three men of Wattleburg, Miles, True, and Casper, approach Miles's wife, Dorothy, for her consent to be in the show, to play her accordion to accompany it, and to use a mortgage payment to support it. Dorothy initially resists participating in the men's "infernal descent," but they insist the play is a "righteous good cause"; after all, it is a "fundraiser" for "the kids for Christmas."[17] Dorothy relents, even if the "fancy freakshow" consists of "lady-clothes, dancing, and gambling all baked in one clove-foot casserole."[18]

Until the end of the play, this is the only scene that takes place in the private sphere of the home—a heteronormative, conventional female space. The stage directions note Dorothy is "busy cooking supper."[19] I suggest Dorothy's opposition and the location of it indicate "the public, overt breach or deliberate nonfulfillment of some crucial norm regulating the intercourse of the parties." This is Turner's definition of the first step of the social drama.[20]

Like the court jesters, holy mendicants, and dharma bums Turner describes in *Ritual Process*, Casper is one of those neophytes who "fall in the interstices of social structure," live "on its margins," and "occupy its lowest rungs."[21] After one of the Elks Club rehearsals, Casper praises True's acting: "You make a real good woman," he tells him. True is hardly grateful for the compliment about his drag, answering, "I sorta hoped I wouldn't be any good . . . Like that'd mean I was a real man." Casper responds, "You're the realest man I know." True leaves the room.[22]

After another rehearsal, as the two men talk in the dressing room, Casper lays his head on True's shoulder. True does not shrug him off and instead produces a postcard of Mary Pickford, telling Casper, "Must be hard, growing up here with no one to look at. You just take her outta your pocket once a day [and] you'll be fine."[23] True suggests daily masturbation ought to cure what ails Casper. In performance, the scene can be heartbreaking.

Alone and sighing ("True and Casper, Casper and True"), Casper starts to apply his stage makeup, practicing his lines as Greta, the maid; it seems a comfort to him. Over the course of the monologue, his manner and makeup evolve until, at the end of the monologue, he is Greta through and through.[24] This moment marks the beginning of the crisis or margin, during which "ritual subjects pass through a period and area of ambiguity, a sort of social limbo which has few (though sometimes these are most crucial) of the attributes of either the preceding or subsequent profane social status or cultural states."[25]

The monologue Casper rehearses is from Valentino's letter to the maid: "How you must die a little death every time you conceal your desire. Forever unable to say your love, a love forbidden by society" (figure 1). There is a knock at the door, and "Greta hides the letter in her décolletage." The playwright refers to the character only as "Greta" and with the physical gesture brings our attention to "her" womanly, if not female, body. Greta answers the door; the stage directions read: "Someone who looks just like Casper enters the room, dressed in male clothing. It is the actress who played the director Zina, now playing Casper."[26] "Sexlessness and anonymity," Turner writes in *Ritual Process*, "are highly characteristic of liminality. In many kinds of initiation where the neophytes are of both sexes, males and females are dressed alike and referred to by the same term."[27] In the reality of the play, Casper has entered his dressing room and found Greta there. In the reality of the performance, the actress who was playing the lesbian director Zina has come onstage dressed as Casper and met the actor who was playing Casper and now plays Greta. Casper (gendered man, sexed woman) asks Greta (gendered woman, sexed man):

Figure 1. Steven Boyer as Casper/Greta in the 2006 production at the Humana Festival of New American Plays at Actors Theatre of Louisville (http://www.kristonedesign.com). Courtesy of Kris Stone.

> CASPER: But if you're Greta—and I'm here—and you're there . . . then who am I?
> GRETA: That is the eternal question, Monsieur Casper.
> CASPER (To himself): Who *am* I?[28]

This confusion is typical of liminaries who "are betwixt-and-between established states of politico-jural structure"—a structure we see in the kitchen at the beginning of the play. "They evade ordinary cognitive classification, too, for they are neither-this-nor-that, here-nor-there, one-thing-not-the-other."[29] Later, Greta will answer Casper's question: "What a curious in-between creature you are!"[30]

Moe Meyer borrows Linda Hutcheon's understanding of parody as "the total body of performative practices and strategies used to enact a queer identity."[31] For Hutcheon, parody reveals "a crisis in the entire notion of the subject as a coherent and continuous source of signification."[32] That crisis is how Eve Sedgwick connotes queerness: "The open mesh of possibilities, gaps, overlaps, dissonances and resonances, lapses and excesses of meaning when the constituent elements of anyone's gender or anyone's sexuality aren't made (or can't be made) to signify monolithically."[33] Queer, in other words, marks what Turner refers to as the "'dramatic time'" (a phrase Turner himself places in quotation marks) that "has replaced routinized social living."[34] It is metatheatricality.

Unlike in more conventional plays-within-plays, like *The Rehearsal* or *Noises Off*, in *Act a Lady* we never discover the title of the play sponsored by the Elks. Either it is unknowable, or it is fully knowable as *Act a Lady*: as Harrison's *Act a Lady* progresses, it is consumed by the play *Act a Lady* the Elks rehearse. After all, Turner describes the liminal crisis "as extremely 'contagious'" with "some of the characteristics of plague."[35]

In *From Ritual to Theatre*, Turner defines antistructure as the "liberation of human capacities for cognition, affect, volition, creativity, etc., from the normative constraints incumbent upon occupying a sequence of social statuses, enacting a multiplicity of social roles."[36] The play-within-the-play takes over the play, and the characters within take over the characters without, as with Casper and Greta, the actor and the acted. While the liminaries here may become structurally invisible, as Turner suggests,[37] they become antistructurally visible, as they "elude and slip through the network of classifications that normally locate states and positions in cultural space."[38] Turner's choice of words recalls David Savran's connotation of queer: "'Queer' remains a useful way for thinking about an American theater in which . . . ostensibly stable meanings and identities (sexual or otherwise) are routinely displaced by notions of mutability, instability, and polyvalence."[39] It may come as no surprise that Casper shares his name with a famous friendly ghost; indeed, "ghosts" is one term Victor Turner uses to describe those in the liminal stage.[40]

Throughout the first act, Harrison indicates that a red curtain appears for the rehearsals of the eighteenth-century scenes (figure 2). In act 2, scene 1, when Valentino and Greta meet, the stage directions read: "The red curtain has tracked off altogether, revealing a more open, less familiar world. Like the forest of a Shakespearean comedy."[41] As with Arden, liminality is a place of "wilderness."[42] Casper and Greta meet again in act 2, scene 8; Casper is still played by the female actor who played Zina, and Greta is still played by the male actor who played Casper. She, played by a man, is outside; he, played by a woman, is inside. Greta despairs about the loss of her beloved Valentino, strangled by Lady Romola's ghost: "But what sunset can I ride into, if not on a stallion's strong back? Will ever man cross my girlish path again?" Casper enters with the stage direction, "[he] crosses her girlish path." When he tries to be aroused by the Pickford postcard, Greta offers to show him "what to do." She embraces Casper: "I give myself over to the nether-reaching roilings!"[43]

Figure 2. Boyer and Paul O'Brien as Miles/Lady Romola in the Humana production (http://www.kristonedesign.com). Courtesy of Kris Stone.

Narratively, Greta selects Casper as a replacement for her lost Valentino. Theatrically, it is the original male actor who tells the same male character he is in love. Moe Meyer writes: "In that case, parody becomes the process whereby the marginalized and disenfranchised advance their own interests by entering alternative signifying codes into the discourse by attaching them to existing structures of signification."[44] The "original" is the Casper of act 1, the one with a "swish" and a "glide" who was given a pinup to treat his homosexuality.[45] Gendered as a woman, opposite a sexed woman playing him, Casper enters into that alternative code. "The open road will put the blush back in your cheek and the roil in your reaches," the original Casper tells the alternative Casper.[46] In effect, the young man is learning to love himself; he just needed a rite of passage to get there. In *The Anthropology of Performance*, Victor Turner wrote, "If man is a sapient animal, a toolmaking animal, a self-making animal, a symbol-using animal, he is, no less, a performing animal . . . his performances are, in a way, *reflexive*, in performing he reveals himself to himself."[47] As the director Zina tells her cast in Wattleburg: "Why have so many attempted this classical tale of becoming? . . . Many have found that the story wakes them from their own drawing rooms, out into the sunlight of self-awareness."[48]

In 1982 Turner noted a "'postmodern turn' in anthropology" that "involves the processualization of space, its temporalization, as against the spatialization of process or time, which we found to be of the essence of the modern."[49] Except for the scenes that frame the play and those in the Arden-like wilderness, *Act a Lady* takes place backstage and in dressing rooms—the loci of theatrical process and becoming. Frank Browning writes in *A Queer Geography*: "Our change, engineered at once through confrontation and seduction, is genuinely shamanic: it is not to protect ourselves, but to subvert certainty and to destabilize power; it is not to build new families, but to open up and nurture the queer spaces already inside them; it is not to retreat into our own safe space, but to discover, protect and electrify the queer zones in calcified, dispirited communities everywhere."[50]

At the end of the coda, True, who (heteronormatively) used the prop emerald as an engagement token to the play's costume designer, ends this act too with another (queerer) gift to Casper. He "takes off the emerald and puts it around Casper's neck."[51] After the liminal phase, during reincorporation, "the ritual subject," Turner writes, "is in a relatively stable state once more and, by virtue of this, has rights and obligations vis-à-vis others of a clearly defined 'structural' type."[52]

In *Still Acting Gay*, John M. Clum asserts, "Only when a character has embarked on such a self-creation can he forge relationships that meaningfully and honestly connect him to other people."[53] Tom Lee was only given tea and some sympathy behind a locked door; in *Act a Lady*, "Casper holds up the emerald and it glistens in the light. Simultaneously, they all whistle at it."[54] A re-formed *communitas*, Harrison's characters have all felt the authentic power of the faux emerald. In *The Anthropology of Performance*, Turner described the breach in social drama as "altruistic."[55] Indeed, as one critic has noted of Harrison's play, "This transformation is the playwright's gift to Casper, and to us."[56]

Notes

Special thanks to Noreen C. Barnes and Aaron D. Anderson for their comments on earlier versions of this article.

1. Robert Anderson, *Tea and Sympathy* (New York: Random House, 1953), 173.

2. Eve Kosofsky Sedgwick, *Epistemology of the Closet* (Berkeley: University of California Press, 1990), 1.

3. John M. Clum, *Still Acting Gay: Male Homosexuality in Modern Drama* (New York: St. Martin's, 2000), 207.

4. Ibid., 156.

5. Victor Turner, *From Ritual to Theatre: The Human Seriousness of Play* (New York: PAJ Publications, 1982), 12.

6. Ibid., 13.

7. Ibid., 10.

8. Victor Turner, "Variations on a Theme of Liminality," in *Secular Ritual*, ed. Sally F. Moore and Barbara G. Myerhoff (Assen, The Netherlands: Van Gorcum, 1977), 46.

9. Turner, *From Ritual to Theatre*, 41.

10. Ibid., 46.

11. Moe Meyer, "Reclaiming the Discourse of Camp," in *Queer Cinema, the Film Reader*, ed. Harry Benshoff and Sean Griffin (New York: Routledge, 2004), 138.

12. Laurence Senelick, "The Queer Root of Theater," in *The Queerest Art: Essays on Lesbian and Gay Theater*, ed. Alisa Solomon and Framji Minwalla (New York: New York University Press, 2002), 25.

13. Eli Rozik, *The Roots of Theatre: Rethinking Ritual and Other Theories of Origin* (Iowa City: University of Iowa Press, 2002), 11.

14. Dick Hebdige. *Subculture: The Meaning of Style* (London: Routledge, 1979), 2.

15. Ibid., 85–86.

16. Victor Turner, *Dramas, Fields, and Metaphors: Symbolic Action in Human Society* (Ithaca, NY: Cornell University Press, 1974), 41.

17. Jordan Harrison, *Act a Lady* (New York: Playscripts, 2006), 12–13.

18. Ibid., 14–15.

19. Ibid., 11.

20. Turner, *Dramas, Fields, and Metaphors*, 38.

21. Victor Turner, *The Ritual Process: Structure and Anti-Structure* (Chicago: Aldine, 1969), 125.

22. Harrison, *Act a Lady*, 28.

23. Ibid., 42.

24. Ibid., 43–44.

25. Turner, *From Ritual to Theatre*, 24.

26. Harrison, *Act a Lady*, 44.

27. Turner, *Ritual Process*, 102.

28. Harrison, *Act a Lady*, 45.

29. Turner, "Variations on a Theme of Liminality," 37.

30. Harrison, *Act a Lady*, 62.

31. Meyer, "Reclaiming the Discourse of Camp," 139.

32. Linda Hutcheon, *A Theory of Parody: The Teachings of Twentieth-Century Art Forms* (New York: Methuen, 1985), 4–5.

33. Eve Kosofsky Sedgwick, *Tendencies* (Durham, NC: Duke University Press, 1993), 8.

34. Turner, *From Ritual to Theatre*, 9.

35. Victor Turner, *The Anthropology of Performance* (New York: PAJ Publications, 1988), 103.

36. Turner, *From Ritual to Theatre*, 44.

37. Turner, "Variations on a Theme of Liminality," 37.

38. Turner, *Ritual Process*, 95.

39. David Savran, "Queer Theater and the Disarticulation of Identity," in Solomon and Minwalla, *The Queerest Art*, 154.

40. Turner, *From Ritual to Theatre*, 27.

41. Harrison, *Act a Lady*, 48.

42. Turner, *Ritual Process*, 95.

43. Harrison, *Act a Lady*, 61–63.

44. Meyer, "Reclaiming the Discourse of Camp," 144.

45. Harrison, *Act a Lady*, 32.

46. Ibid., 63.

47. Turner, *Anthropology of Performance*, 81.

48. Harrison, *Act a Lady*, 20.

49. Turner, *Anthropology of Performance*, 76.

50. Frank Browning, *A Queer Geography: Journeys Toward a Sexual Self* (New York: Crown, 1996), 35.

51. Harrison, *Act a Lady*, 78.

52. Turner, *Ritual Process*, 95.

53. Clum, *Still Acting Gay*, 198.

54. Harrison, *Act a Lady*, 78.

55. Turner, *Anthropology of Performance*, 38.

56. Deborah Stein, "Jordan Harrison, Making Language Necessary," *Brooklyn Rail*, December 2007, accessed March 11, 2012, http://brooklynrail.org/2007/12/theater/jordan-harrison-making-language-necessary.

Clash with the Vikings

Gerpla and the Struggle for
National Identity in Iceland

Steve Earnest

SINCE FORMALLY gaining its independence from Denmark in 1944, the island nation of Iceland has struggled with its Viking legacy. This history—a history rooted in barbarianism, primitive customs, and the worship of pagan gods—sharply contrasts with the nature of contemporary Iceland. Characterized by high ideals and intellectual mores, advanced artistic levels, and very sophisticated standards of living, contemporary Iceland generally rejects its barbaric past in favor of peace, Christianity, and high cultural standards. Prior to the financial collapse of 2008, which saw the failure of Iceland's three major banks, the standard of living in Iceland ranked among the highest in the world in terms of societal data such as quality of education, health care, social care, and other social systems. However, the economic crash in Iceland in 2008 has been classified as the largest suffered by any country relative to the size of its economy.[1]

In 2010, the National Theatre of Iceland undertook a major project to address the question of national identity in Iceland, considering why and how the financial collapse happened, how Iceland would recover, and the country's relationship with its Viking heritage. Using Halldór Laxness's 1952 novel *Gerpla* as the framework for this question, the National Theatre sought to create a work viewing Iceland's history and mythology through a contemporary lens. This essay will analyze the National Theatre's production of *Gerpla*, which explored Iceland's nearly one-thousand-year history, by examining the rituals and background of Iceland's history from the perspective of postcollapse Iceland in 2010.

The works of Nobel laureate Halldór Laxness (1902–1998) have been adapted often for the stage throughout Europe and have generally presented a balanced view of Iceland's long and frequently difficult history. In *Iceland's Bell*, produced by the National Theatre of Iceland in early 2008, Laxness tells the story of Jon Hreggvidsson, a man convicted of theft for stealing a fishing line to feed his family. After numerous unsuccessful appeals, the petty crime escalates to international proportions; Hreggvidsson is taken to Copenhagen for a final appeal to the king of Denmark. At that point the story becomes a symbol of Iceland's struggle for independence from Denmark. According to Tinna Gunnlaugsdottir, artistic director of the National Theatre of Iceland, "The leading lady of the play, Snaefridur Eydalin, is a symbol for Iceland and she is in love with a man who is collecting all of the old books in Iceland and bringing them to Copenhagen to preserve them but at the same time he is stripping the country of its culture. So we did this play and it was highly successful for more than two years and I think it's because it . . . [had opened just before] the collapse happened. The work took on a new meaning as it asked the question: where are we now that the money has lost its value—what value do we stand for, who are we, and what set of values should you associate us with?"[2]

The production of *Iceland's Bell* paved the way for *Gerpla*, a work that arguably provided the most significant commentary on Icelandic history the country had seen. Staged by renowned Icelandic stage and film director Balthasar Kormárkur on the main stage of the National Theatre, *Gerpla* remained in the repertory for over a year and won the 2010 Grimàn award for Best Icelandic Production. The play attempts to present and reenvision Iceland's past by employing and commenting on the form of the Icelandic saga, addressing ideals of the Vikings and the barbarian "poet/fighter," and commenting on contemporary brutality and behavior patterns that ultimately led to Iceland's financial collapse in 2008.

First, the text of Laxness's novel should be considered. The title *Gerpla* loosely translates as "The Happy Warriors," a play on the Icelandic Viking tradition and a parody of the Icelandic saga, a traditional Scandinavian epic form that combines both narrative and dramatic action with fact and fiction. Icelandic sagas provide much of the source material detailing the history of medieval Icelandic life. However, the sagas often glorify acts of brutality, violence, and plundering; indeed, one theory holds that the word "Viking" is derived from the word *vicar* ("to plunder").[3] For example, one of the most famous sagas is *Njal's Saga*, which details the gory events of a fifty-year blood feud in medieval Iceland and includes acts such as the capture and eventual enslavement of victims from Ireland and the United Kingdom. In *Njal's Saga*, the captured men are put to work and the women are initially raped and later made servants for the Viking masters. It is generally believed that Viking plundering began around AD 780, when inhabitants of Saint Cuthbert's Monastery on the Island of Lindisfarne on the northern coast of the United Kingdom were captured and taken to Iceland.[4] Historically, Iceland was also useful to the Vikings as a "prison" for captives due to its unusual geography and relative isolation.

Laxness's novel is a parody of *Fóstbræðra Saga* (literally "Foster Brother's Saga") and the sagas in general and is written in a style similar to that of the sagas. Laxness mocks the ideal, held at the time by most of his fellow Icelanders, of the Vikings as heroic warrior-poets who represented high ideals and literary standards. He paints the Vikings as idiots and ruffians whose ultimate demise is brought about by a penchant for springing to violence at every opportunity. For example, one of the two main characters, Þorgeir Hávarsson, is a violent sociopath who regards the inattention of a deaf and blind man as a sign of disrespect and kills the man as punishment. The other principal character, Þormóður Bessarson, dreams of one day being a great poet, recording the feats of his friend Þorgeir and his hero, the Norwegian would-be king Ólafur Haraldsson (a historical figure and precursor to European dictators of the twentieth century). Þormóður, however, is also a violent thug who continually asserts that killing and conquering are far more valuable pastimes than fishing or other menial tasks.

The dramatic text of *Gerpla* includes numerous references to the violent nature of the Viking lifestyle. In the first scene of the play, an unnamed young girl discovers the severed head of Þorgeir on a stake outside her house. The play then shifts back thirty years and takes the audience on a journey through the lives of Þorgeir and his cousin Þormóður, two would-be warriors who find themselves caught up in events of the thirteenth century. Through a storyteller, *Gerpla* explores the tale of Þorgeir and Þormóður in episodic fashion, jumping through time on numerous occasions. Within the first one hundred lines of the play, the storyteller describes in graphic detail how to cut a man in half:

> The skull is surprisingly strong and can endure heavy blows. Its strength is derived from its dome shape, much as the dome of a cathedral. But when a powerful blow comes together in one place it can give way. Then the strength of the skull falters and splits. The skull is carried by seven vertebrae, aligned between the torso and the head. Between the vertebrae are sacks of liquid that are easy to sever. Therefore the best place to cut a man in two is the neck. If you cut past the neck and spine the next stop is the collar bone or the shoulder, then we may consider the man split down the center.[5]

Historically, Vikings used decapitation and the display of severed heads to terrorize opponents and to frighten them into submission. Later in the text there are repeated statements by Þorgeir that compare everyday life to that of the warrior: "It is unworthy of free men to be submitted to pulling fish out of the water and tending sheep, instead of raising wealth by war and good man slaying."[6] Essentially, the two would-be warriors represent the Viking mentality of conquest, terrorism, and plunder.

Though the Vikings initially worshipped only Norse gods, they began to accept Christianity around AD 1250. In *Gerpla*, the reaction to the introduction of Christ into Iceland is handled violently by Þorgeir and Þormóður through their confrontation with a Christ-follower named Jorund. The scene plays as follows:

> ÞORGEIR: We have heard that Christ is a coward and will not fight.
> JORUND: Are you unbaptized men?
> ÞORGEIR: I know not what the wretch asked us. Answer this instead, where was the white Christ's greatest battle?
> JORUND: He rose up from the dead and was never livelier than then. This was his greatest fight.
> ÞORGEIR: How did he treat his enemies, when he had leapt from the cross?
> JORUND: Though Christ was crucified by evildoers and pierced with a spear, none could keep him in Hell longer than he wanted to stay. And when he was resurrected he made all men his sons, both good and evil.
> ÞORMÓÐUR: How many women had he?
> JORUND: Men's and women's souls sprang from his forehead in the Kingdom of Heaven and prayed at his feet, while he was enthroned in joy before the kingdom of the world.
> ÞORGEIR: My mother has told me that the only true words are those that ride on swords.
> JORUND: Greater than slaying men, was the victory of the Virgin's son, when he made all mankind his equals, giving each man a soul, creating thralls as well as kings from the same fabric.[7]

The two thugs proceed to beat the missionary, threatening to bash in his skull if he keeps proselytizing on the island (figure 1).

The two cousins and oath-brothers engage in a continuing path of violence and terrorism, their ultimate goal being the instillation of fear in the hearts of all who hear their names. Late in the play Þorgeir states: "Many a dark night while others have slept have I risen from my bed, raised my weapons, and bit the shield rim in an uncontrollable thirst for the praise that is won by killing men and ruling the world, or dying in glory. I have heard that there is in the Jokulfjords a mighty champion named Butraldi, son of Brusi, that claims he fears no man. Such a cham-

Figure 1. Þorgeir and Þormóður beat a Christ-follower. *Gerpla*, produced by the National Theatre of Iceland (þjóðleikhúsið), February 2012. Courtesy of Eggert Thor Jonsson.

pion will be no small threat to us, while he is alive. My counsel is that we should sail out against him this night, make him our enemy and fight him until the end."[8] They defeat and kill Butraldi, but their continued violence results in their banishment from Iceland as Christianity begins to take hold.

In the end, the two part ways. Þormóður becomes weary of plundering and decides to become a farmer and marry a young girl named Thordis, who bears him two sons. Þorgeir sails to Norway to become a servant to his idol, King Olaf. Years later, Olaf sends Þorgeir back to Iceland with the express purpose of killing Icelanders, but after the long journey from Norway, Þorgeir is killed by two "petty men" who find him dozing in his tent in the middle of the day and behead him in his sleep. Þorgeir's head is returned to his home on a stake, an act that in the context of Laxness's story signals the end of the Viking Age in Iceland and brings the play full circle.

Attempting to comment on the whole of Icelandic society, including the soul of the Icelandic people as well as intellectual ideas and a masculine physicality, director Kormárkur employed a movement and costuming style based on two ancient Icelandic sources: Icelandic wrestling and

the ancient form of Viking dance known as *vikivaki*. Icelandic wrestling
is a sport dating from the Viking period. Actors in the production wore
traditional Icelandic wrestling uniforms, known as *glima*, to emphasize
the surge in Icelandic nationalism following World War II. The vikivaki
dance style is associated with the worship of pagan gods and has been
traced as one of the primary sources of performance in medieval Iceland.[9]
The references to traditional Viking forms of dance and wrestling, along
with the use of the form of Icelandic saga, reinforced the development
of national identity through national symbols, rituals, and literary material.

Because both Icelandic wrestling and vikivaki have been practiced from
medieval times (since around AD 1100) until today, Kormárkur felt that
their use would be critical in the creation of a unifying form for the Icelandic audience. From the very beginning of the piece, the performers
used movement to tell the dense story in the saga form. For example, as
the play opened, the actors spelled out the word "Gerpla," contorting
their bodies using glima and vikivaki and various movements and patterns (figure 2). The performers began in a circle, eventually breaking
into pairs that symbolized the opposites of fire and ice that have continually characterized Iceland.[10] Similarly, the use of glima involved two participants "securing the waist of the opponent and either picking them
up in order to slam them onto the ground and then pinning their back
onto the ground for a period of two to three seconds."[11] This clumsy,
rough combination of artistic movement and brutal fighting drove the
play. While it often placed considerable demands on the timing, it ultimately characterized the work as intrinsically Icelandic.

Kormárkur also incorporated Asian theatre techniques (reinforc-
ing the use of a contemporary, "Brechtian" lens). Visible onstage assis-
tants, dressed in black, manipulated objects attached to sticks that were
"thrown" in slow motion during fight sequences. This slow-motion technique created a theatrical representation of medieval Viking warriors
while simultaneously establishing a contemporary theatrical sensibility.

Director Kormárkur had much to say about *Gerpla*. In an interview in
December 2011, he noted:

> I thought *Gerpla* is probably, like *Peer Gynt*, an important national story
> for Iceland. It was a new era in my directing career after I came back from
> film. I felt that after I started directing movies, like a movie director in a
> prison. So it was blending into my work as a stage director, or a frustrated
> film director making plays. But after I did films and had success, I felt freed.
> I could now do theatre on its own, there was no movie making in my theatre
> any more, I could make theatre on its own, I started working more closely
> with actors and in improvisation and then I threw a book on the table (of

Figure 2. Use of *vikivaki* and *glíma*. *Gerpla*, produced by the National Theatre of Iceland (Þjóðleikhúsið), February 2012. Courtesy of Eggert Thor Jonsson.

course I do my homework and all that) and said let's make a play . . . I did not decide too much in advance, I wanted to create it with a group of actors and it was because the film world is all about organizing—every minute is so expensive—and it's more difficult to do something spontaneous and react to what people do.[12]

Gerpla reinforced to the Icelandic people the view that the Vikings were bumbling, violent morons who spread their plundering across the northern seas for nothing more than economic gain and macho bragging rights. Kormárkur noted that the behavior of the marauding, invading Vikings of the Middle Ages was exactly the same as was being seen by Icelandic investors and bankers in the early 2000s, sailing out into world markets with the goal of bringing back huge wealth to Iceland as well as personal gain: "So maybe a play like *Gerpla* . . . reaches our core. . . . Way back they [were] saying that we have to go abroad and win countries and win battles and capture things and become famous and this is exactly what happened just before the financial collapse."[13]

The Viking era was more than a historical period: it forged the basic characteristics of the Icelandic people both positively and negatively. However, the Viking legacy ultimately led to a colossal failure. While many Icelandic theatre companies chose to comment on this failure by presenting contemporary plays (for example, the Reykjavik City Theatre presented the musical *Enron* as well as *The Cherry Orchard* and other modern works), Kormárkur felt that only a work by an Icelandic author deeply rooted in Icelandic history could truly get to the root of the problem. Ultimately, this is true not only from the standpoint of content but also of form. Because of both the content and form of *Gerpla* (the novel and the play), it certainly had more resonance with an Icelandic audience than did productions of American or British works espousing ideas regarding financial collapse. Additionally, since the work included the stylistic element of stage movement based on traditional Icelandic forms, it can be argued that the ultimate goal of the production was nothing less than to theatricalize a thousand years of Icelandic culture. The artistic director of the National Theatre of Iceland, Tinna Gunnlaugsdottir, comments:

> We can go into our Viking period, but a play like *Gerpla*, that can go further and use that heritage as a starting point and make it more [theatrical] and I think that this is a sacred area to go into. . . . Balthasar's production was controversial because . . . it's kind of sacred but there is so much there—there is so much theatre in the sagas, it is so compact and of course you cannot do so many big fights on stage but you can find a solution, a way to present them theatrically. That fits the stage. But . . . I think we need to see theatre using our heritage and I think that Balthasar proved that you can do this through *Gerpla*—it is something that you can put on stage if you use the conditions of the theatre not the book.[14]

In the end, the National Theatre of Iceland's production of *Gerpla* was a theatrical experiment that fell short of its lofty goal to stage an incredibly detailed saga. While there was value in seeing the events onstage that Laxness pulled from medieval saga texts, the realities of dramatic form gave audiences little more than a "highlight reel" of a work of much larger scope. *Gerpla* was significant in the sense that it gave physical form to the actions, movements, and personalities of its Viking characters and allowed the Icelandic public to confront a huge part of its national history. Because most Icelanders attend theatre regularly and travel to Reykjavik to do so, it is conceivable that as much as 75 percent of the nation attended this production. For an island nation of just over three hundred thousand inhabitants, this was an important component in a process of national healing.

Notes

1. "Iceland: Cracks in the Crust," *The Economist*, December 11, 2008.
2. Interview with Tinna Gunnlaugsdottir, artistic director, National Theatre of Iceland, December 2011.

3. "Icelandic Vikings—Vikings in Iceland," Explore Iceland, accessed April 2012, http://www.exploreiceland.is/about_iceland/history_of_iceland/icelandic_vikings/.

4. Ibid.

5. Balthsar Komárkur, "Gerpla" (unpublished dramatic text, 2010), National Theatre of Iceland.

6. Ibid.

7. Ibid.

8. Ibid.

9. Svienn Einarsson, *A People's Theatre Comes of Age: Icelandic Theatre, 1860–1920* (Reykjavik: University of Iceland Press, 2008).

10. Terry Gunnell, "Waking the 'Wiggle-Waggle' Monsters (Animal Figures and Cross Dressing in the Icelandic Vikivaki Games)," unpublished manuscript, Folk Drama Studies Today Panel at the International Traditional Drama Conference, University of Sheffield, England, July 19–21, 2002.

11. Interview with Jón Vidar Jónsson, curator of the Theatre Museum, Reykjavik, Iceland, December 2011.

12. Komárkur, "Gerpla."

13. Interview with Balthasar Komárkur, director and coauthor of *Gerpla*, Reykjavik, Iceland, December 2011.

14. Interview with Tinna Gunnlaugsdottir, artistic director, National Theatre of Iceland, December 2011.

Heaven and Earth

Confession as Performance in *Hamlet* and *Measure for Measure*

Jennifer Flaherty

STAGED CONFESSIONS function as performances for two audiences: the earthly audience of paying spectators and the heavenly audience of God. In *Measure for Measure* and *Hamlet*, both written around the turn of the seventeenth century, Shakespeare makes the decision to stage the confessions of the plays' two villains, Angelo and Claudius. In both plays, Shakespeare draws a distinction between the Catholic practice of giving confession in the presence of a priest and the Protestant form of addressing God directly. He also juxtaposes heavenly and earthly law by presenting a series of practical questions and conflicts comparing religious and legal modes of confession. Shakespeare's plays do not present confession as a simple process of contrition and forgiveness. Instead, both *Measure for Measure* and *Hamlet* present the ritual as a complex process that is difficult to understand or perform properly; the innocent and guilty alike struggle to distinguish between the sacred and the secular in their efforts to achieve absolution.

Shakespeare was not the first playwright to introduce confession to the English stage. The sacrament was a staple of medieval morality plays, most notably *The Summoning of Everyman* in the late fifteenth century. *Everyman* presents the sacrament as a clearly defined and accessible way to avoid Purgatory and damnation. When Everyman is encouraged by Knowledge and Good Deeds to confess his sins, he leaves the stage confident of his ability to complete the sacrament, saying: "Now of penaunce I wyll wade the water clere,/ To saue me from Purgatory, that sharpe fyre."[1] Everyman's penance mirrors the Catholic sacrament, which is composed of three parts: contrition, confession, and satisfaction.[2] After

Everyman acknowledges his own guilt and confesses his sins, absolution is conveyed to him by a holy representative of God.

With England's break from the Catholic Church, however, the procedure of confessing one's sins to a priest that is glorified in *Everyman* was abolished in favor of a contrition process that emphasized a more personal communication with God. Under Henry VIII, theologian Richard Morison argued against the idea that a priest's absolution could stand in for God's, stating that confession required only the joining of contrition and faith.[3] As David Beauregard explains, the English Reformation reimagined the sacrament as "a purely interior form consisting of four parts or movements: contrition, confession, faith, and amendment of life. Confession was made to God, not a priest."[4]

With the establishment of the Church of England, the monarch became both the sacred and secular leader, the head of both Church and State. In *Hamlet*, Shakespeare begins to explore the precarious transition between achieving the satisfaction of reconciliation through communication with a priest and the more complex process of communicating directly to God through faith and amendment of life. The problematic relationship between heaven and earth is personified in Claudius, who is both sinner and king, both an offender against heaven and an authority on earth. This is especially apparent in Claudius's confession scene, in which he attempts to combine contrition, confession, faith, and amendment before a triple audience (God, of whom he is aware, and Hamlet and the theater audience, of whom he is not). In a play about inaction, this scene focuses on two aborted actions: Claudius's confession and Hamlet's unattempted assassination of Claudius. The play investigates the relationship between crimes and divine and earthly justice, exploring the appropriate response to sin.

Claudius begins his confession (or lack thereof) by stating, "My offense is rank: it smells to Heaven."[5] Through these lines the "something rotten"[6] is named. Claudius has sinned against the State by killing the king and taking his crown and has sinned against God and nature by killing his brother and taking his wife. His crime bridges the space between the sacred and the secular, corrupting both the earthly state of Denmark and the heavenly state of his soul. Unlike Everyman, Claudius has no confessor to help him turn his contrition into proper confession to achieve absolution; he remains trapped between his heavenly aspirations and his earthly ambitions:

My fault is past. But, O, what form of prayer
Can serve my turn? 'Forgive me my foul murder'?

That cannot be; since I am still possess'd
Of those effects for which I did the murder,
My crown, mine own ambition and my queen.
May one be pardon'd and retain the offence?[7]

His intention to heal his soul is thwarted by his desire to retain the earthly prizes of his crime; without renouncing his crown and his queen, Claudius cannot hope to achieve the final act of amendment of life. Therefore, Claudius's confession (like his crime and his victim) remains trapped between heaven and earth; this is reinforced at the end of the scene, when he laments, "My words fly up, my thoughts remain below: Words without thoughts never to heaven go."[8]

While we are not given God's response to the confession, Claudius believes his spiritual confession to be a failure. As an authority on the corruption of earthly law, Claudius is able to effectively draw a contrast between the laws of heaven and earth. He argues that his "words without thoughts" can never be successful due to the rigidity of heavenly law:

In the corrupted currents of this world
Offence's gilded hand may shove by justice,
And oft 'tis seen the wicked prize itself
Buys out the law: but 'tis not so above;
There is no shuffling, there the action lies
In his true nature; and we ourselves compell'd,
Even to the teeth and forehead of our faults,
To give in evidence.[9]

Claudius prefers the laxity of earthly justice, which is so steeped in corruption that prisoners can buy their way out of sentences and even an offender like Claudius can serve as an authority, using his ill-gotten gains to avoid discovery and punishment. Claudius struggles more with the idea of heavenly justice, though, explaining that there is no "shuffling" before a divine judge and that the evidence comes in the actions and characters of the defendant. Even in his metaphors here, however, Claudius still confuses heavenly with earthly justice. In both Catholic and Protestant theology, "shuffling" is allowed in the form of contrition and reconciliation. The evidence that Claudius dreads could be offered freely in the form of confession.

The conflict between earthly and heavenly justice is complicated and intensified by Hamlet, who witnesses Claudius's confession. Unlike the viewing audience (and God, presumably), Hamlet misreads the confession, believing it to be successful. As Hamlet contemplates killing Claudius in the confessional, he realizes that the earthly aspect of

Claudius's crime would be addressed and answered with Claudius's death. A king's death and a stolen crown could be balanced by a usurper's death and a crown restored. It is the heavenly aspect of the crime that confuses Hamlet, as it does Claudius. He argues that Claudius's ascent to heaven after dying in the confessional would not balance his father's time in Purgatory: "A villain kills my father; and for that, / I, his sole son, do this same villain send to heaven. / O, this is hire and salary, not revenge."[10]

To achieve true revenge on Claudius, Hamlet must do more than put a stop to Claudius's physical life; he must prevent Claudius's spiritual absolution to balance earthly justice with the heavenly. In this scene, both Claudius and Hamlet lack the context or guidance to properly address heavenly crimes or administer divine justice. Charged with the task of addressing God directly, Claudius finds himself unable to break away from earth. Similarly, Hamlet is unable to properly address the earthly crimes without being distracted by the spiritual implications of his retribution. Claudius's staged confession and Hamlet's reaction bring the theoretical debates about the sacrament to a practical dilemma: How can one achieve heavenly absolution without losing earthly authority?

While Claudius's confession occurs in only a single scene, Shakespeare builds on the contrast between heavenly and earthly confession in *Measure for Measure* (believed to be written a few years after *Hamlet*) by including several such scenes throughout the play. Where Claudius understands the depth of his sin but struggles with the path to absolution, the characters in *Measure for Measure* cannot even agree about what constitutes sin. Through the staged confession scenes, both legal and spiritual, the characters ponder not only how to achieve absolution, but whether sin itself begins with intention or action. The line between terrestrial and celestial law is blurred from the beginning of the first act, when the duke of Vienna takes a brief leave of absence from his position as secular authority and disguises himself as a friar (a spiritual authority) in order to evaluate the performance of his second-in-command, Angelo. When Angelo attempts to establish *his* moral authority by arresting a young man named Claudio for impregnating his fiancée before the marriage, the lines between the sacred and the secular blur even further. Claudio, in need of a virtuous advocate to defend his sin against Angelo's charge of lechery, calls in his sister Isabella, a novice of the order of Saint Clare.

The significance that Isabella attaches to Claudio's sin is a powerful obstacle for her; she cannot make a case for his pardon on the basis that his sin should be overlooked. She is the only character in the play that cannot do so; the lack of gravity in the transgression is well noted in the text. Even Angelo admits that Claudio's sin is useful to him because it is easily apparent and makes a good example, not because it is severe. The duke and Escalus, two characters at least ostensibly characterized by love of justice and knowledge of the law, both argue that the law is too harsh in this particular case and that Claudio's sentence is not appropriate to his crime. Isabella, however, is considering not the laws of earth but the laws of Heaven. According to Paul's epistle to the Romans, death is an apt punishment for Claudio's transgression against God. He is guilty of "being filled with all unrighteousness, fornication . . . knowing the judgment of God, that they which commit such things are worthy of death, not only do the same, but have pleasure in them that do them."[11] Isabella is in the unenviable position of being (apparently) the only one in Vienna who believes that her brother's death is a suitable consequence of his sin while being driven by her love for him to plead for his release. The best argument she can manage under these circumstances is that Angelo should "condemn the fault, and not the actor of it."[12] Such an argument is fitting when one is dealing with crimes against God. It is, in fact, the founding principle of the sacrament of confession, in which individuals can allow their faults to die while they themselves are absolved of them. It is, however, an inappropriate case to make regarding a legal crime, as Angelo states. A legal confession does not imply absolution.

Isabella is most comfortable in discourse that references celestial values and principles; her primary attacks on Angelo are those that condemn him for not living up to a heavenly standard of justice and mercy. In contrast, Angelo's speeches are about terrestrial law; each time that Isabella invokes God to prove her points or illustrate his own weaknesses, Angelo's arguments pull her back to earth. Responding to Angelo's description of her brother as a "forfeit of law," Isabella reminds Angelo that "all the souls there were, were forfeit once."[13] When Isabella laments her brother's lack of time to prepare himself properly to meet his heavenly judge, Angelo responds by turning her attention to the earthly court before her, arguing that terrestrial law "hath slept . . . and future evils . . . are to have no successive degrees."[14] Like the play itself, the two debaters are caught between the laws of God and men, and although they both display a powerful mastery of rhetoric, neither seems to respond in a manner that exactly answers the opposing argument once the topic shifts away from the nature of the sin at hand.

After looking upon her and listening to her argument, Angelo not only understands the sin of lechery, he is willing to partake in it. At the end of their debate, Isabella asks Angelo to "go to your bosom, knock there, and ask your heart what it doth know that's like my brother's fault."[15] Angelo's line at the end of the scene implies that before this scene, such a knock would have gone unanswered; it is the contact with her virtue that has led to his vice. Thus "Lord Angelo—a man of stricture and firm abstinence" does indeed take on the persona of a sinner during this debate, but not only through a rhetorical strategy.[16] Indeed, according to Abelard and Saint Augustine, who maintain that sin comes not from action, but intention, this moment marks the beginning of Angelo's venture into sin: he begins "entertaining mentally an evil suggestion."[17]

Unlike Isabella, to whom the action of a sin means everything, Shakespeare instead concentrates on the intention of the sin. The audience carefully follows Angelo in his transformation from icy, power-hungry sovereign to hypocritical lecher. Shakespeare illustrates the first moment of temptation, Angelo's attempts to fight the temptation, and, at last, Angelo's firm decision to sin. The second encounter of Isabella and Angelo pushes him closer and closer to the intent to sin, until he tells her, "I have begun, and now I give my sensual race the rein; fit thy consent to my sharp appetite."[18] Hence we see Angelo pass through the Augustinian cycle of sin by "1) entertaining mentally an evil suggestion, 2) taking pleasure in contemplating the evil thought or action suggested, and 3) consenting to accept the thought or undertake the action."[19] Even though the bed trick played by Isabella prevents him from carrying out the sin by committing adultery, Angelo is nonetheless guilty according to the definitions of Augustine, which downplay the actual act. Likewise, Aquinas argues that "a man who, without negligence, believes another man's wife to be his own does not sin in having sex with her."[20] Logic would then dictate that a man who willingly sleeps with his wife, thinking her to be another, would be committing adultery through intention, if not action.

Angelo is exonerated by Isabella in the final act of the play, when she makes the case that because he was prevented from turning his intentions into actions, he is innocent of the crimes. Shakespeare, however, makes Angelo's state of sin easily apparent when he stages Angelo's attempted confession. The confession itself is not heard by the audience: act 2, scene 4 begins with Angelo's recognition that his prayers have failed. Indeed, his brief speech is not a prayer but an acknowledgment of an absence of prayer, much like Claudius's staged confession in *Hamlet.*

The two confession scenes are startlingly similar in language and tone. Both men acknowledge that their earthly sins and ambitions pull their prayers from heaven to earth when Claudius says, "My words fly up, my thoughts remain below,"[21] and Angelo says, "Heaven hath my empty words, whilst my invention, hearing not my tongue, anchors on Isabel."[22] Where Claudius declares, "Pray can I not, though inclination be as sharp as will: My stronger guilt defeats my strong intent,"[23] Angelo echoes "Heaven in my mouth, as if I did but only chew his name, and in my heart the strong and swelling evil of my conception."[24] Neither character is presented with a priest or mediator to help him through the process, and both characters struggle to determine the extent of their guilt and the path to absolution.

Like his arguments in his earlier scene with Isabella, all of Angelo's thoughts are tied to the earth. To emphasize the meaningless nature of a confession whose pure contrition does not reach heaven, the imagery in Angelo's speech is that of a void sacrament of communion. Heaven (and God) are present in his words "as if I did but only chew his name."[25] The blood that is referenced throughout both of Angelo's opening speeches is not the blood of Christ, but his own, earthly and impure.

Angelo's is not the only thwarted confession in the text; when he re-enters his own city, the duke takes on the role of a friar and seeks to serve as confessor to several characters. If the dialogue between Isabella and Angelo is caught between the extremes of heaven and earth, the duke himself emanates a similar dichotomy. Throughout the play he shifts between his true role as a secular authority and his sham role as a man devoted to matters of the spirit. Elizabeth Hansen problematizes the duke's role as confessor to female characters such as Juliet and Mariana, arguing that "in *Measure for Measure*, the confessional subject is formed not so much by the operation of authority on the subject as by the ever-present possibility that . . . hierarchy will collapse into equality, difference into sameness."[26]

To Hansen, the issue is one of gender and subjugation: "In these exchanges where it is impossible to mistake the confessor for the simple interlocutor, as when the Duke 'confesses' Juliet and Mariana, the 'penitent' resists formation as a confessional subject."[27] While it is clear that these confessions are problematic, there is no evidence that these problems arise simply from the hierarchy of gender. To suppose so is to ignore the more problematic confessions that the duke attempts with Claudio and Barnadine. While there are undoubtedly issues of gender and subjugation that appear throughout the play, it is more likely that the duke's awkward role as confessor arises from the complicated relationship between heavenly and earthly authority and heavenly and earthly confession. By posing as a confessor, the duke is conflating two standards of judgment and pardon that, as we can see from Claudius and Hamlet, often refuse to be effectively conflated.

The duke's attempted confession of Juliet illustrates his discomfort in his role as a priest more clearly than it illustrates a tension between male and female subjectivity. Upon seeing Juliet, the duke immediately asks her to repent, and she answers in the affirmative. His response is to tell her, "I'll teach you how you shall arraign your conscience and try your penitence, if it be sound, or hollowly put on."[28] While Hansen states that the duke's speech is "enmesh[ed]" in "male intersubjectivity," which "deflect[s] it from Juliet," she also mentions that "we know that whatever the state of Juliet's penance," it is the confessor's authority that is "hollowly put on."[29] It is more likely that the latter of these two observations is the prominent reason that this confession fails. Juliet's initial reaction to the priest is not to "[resist] formation as a confessional subject."[30] On the contrary, she eagerly confesses, repents, or gives favorable responses in each of her seven lines in the scene: she is the perfect confessional subject. The problems with the scene lie not in the confession, but in the confessor. In his attempt to "teach" Juliet the difference between a false and true repentance, the duke finds that Juliet's responses come more readily than his own questions. Indeed, most of his questions are not those of a ghostly father confessor; they are the questions of a curious earthly duke who wants to understand the case before him and pass judgment. Juliet's answers to his questions do not, in fact, lead to saving her soul, but to saving Claudio's life.

The most problematic, and the most amusing, of the duke's false confessions is his encounter with Barnadine, a prisoner who has been awaiting execution for nine years but has failed to repent. Barnadine's precarious theological state is comparable to that of Hamlet's father at the time of death; without a proper confession, he risks Purgatory or damnation. When Angelo demands Claudio's head despite the efforts of the duke, Mariana, and Isabella to secure his release, Barnadine is called to "rise and be hanged" and the duke is introduced as his "ghostly father," who has "come to advise [him], comfort [him], and pray with [him]."[31] For the duke to pose as confessor to a man soon to be hanged (by the duke's own order) is a far more serious matter than his earlier bit of playacting with Juliet. More startling is Barnadine's own condemnation of the confession itself. He declares that he "will not consent to die this day" due to his own sinful behavior the previous evening and his need for "more time to prepare me."[32] This utter refusal to partake in the process of confession is a far more dramatic attempt on the part of "the 'penitent' [to resist] formation as a confessional subject"[33] than any of Juliet's mildly subversive remarks.

After serving (falsely) as a holy authority throughout most of the play, the duke finally serves as an earthly authority when he presides over Angelo's trial in the final act. With the judgment of Angelo, the play comes full circle. Once again the issue of earthly transgression and punishment comes into conflict with heavenly judgment; once again Isabella must weigh her beliefs against her emotions. Arguing more effectively for Angelo than she did for Claudio, Isabella focuses her speech on action rather than intention with regard to sin. Despite Angelo's entirely sinful intentions, Isabella exonerates him by saying that "for Angelo, his act did not o'ertake his bad intent, and must be buried but as an intent that perished by the way."[34] By negating intentions and focusing on actions, Isabella is able to make her case effectively, but she ignores the mental component of sin in both a heavenly and an earthly context.

"Thoughts are no subjects; intents, but merely thoughts."[35] Isabella concludes her speech to the duke with these words, articulating the philosophy that has informed her actions since the beginning of the play. Her words directly oppose the more intentionalist philosophy of scholars such as Augustine and Abelard, who would have found Angelo guilty. To Augustine, thoughts are far more than "merely thoughts," because "the mind cannot decide both that a sin is to be thought of with pleasure, and also to be carried into effect, unless that intention of the mind which wields the sovereign power of moving the members to action or of restraining them from action also yields to and becomes a slave of the vile deed."[36] The thoughts that Isabella dismisses so quickly are, in Augustine's philosophy, the first step of sin. Although Abelard does state that "to wish is not the same thing as to fulfill a wish. Equally, to sin is not the same as to carry out a sin,"[37] his meaning is that one does not sin if one merely entertains the idea without pursuing the action. It does not follow (for Abelard) that a true intent to sin that has been foiled is sinless.

In her speech, Isabella fails to dwell on Angelo's clear intention to commit the sin, of which she is entirely aware; she dismisses it even more easily than she does his sinful thoughts. Yet it is within his decision to move from contemplating the sin to actively pursuing it that Angelo's sin truly follows the intentionalist view. Randall Curren interprets Augustine's "steps of sin" to mean that "whether any 'bodily action' actually follows from the consent of the will [Augustine] thought irrelevant to whether there was a sin."[38] The moment of fault, for Augustine, lies in "consenting to accept the thought or undertake the action."[39] Likewise, John Marenbon states that "Abelard held that neither the performance of the external act itself, nor any of the thoughts or feelings preceding it but not directly linked to its real or planned performance, need be considered in judging sin."[40] For both theologians, the action to which Isabella attaches so much weight is immaterial. Angelo knows that pursuing Isabella is a sinful act, but he entertains the thought with pleasure, takes pains to set up a rendezvous, and arrives at the designated spot fully prepared to turn thoughts into action. Angelo sins the moment he intends to commit adultery.

When Angelo appears before the duke, he acknowledges his sin, and his legal confession is reminiscent of a spiritual confession:

O my dread lord,
I should be guiltier than my guiltiness
To think I can be undiscernible [*sic*],
When I perceive your Grace, like power divine
Hath looked upon my passes. Then, good prince,
No longer session hold upon my shame,
But let my trial be mine own confession.
Immediate sentence then, and sequent death
Is all the grace I beg.[41]

Derek Cohen states, "There is surely an unintended but biting irony in Angelo's characterization of the Duke as a kind of holy authority when his entire project has been to effect a secular miracle by deception and disguise."[42] This irony might not be unintended. The audience knows that the duke has been posing as a holy emissary (but functioning as an earthly ruler) for most of the play; now, he is presented as an earthly ruler and praised as a holy emissary. But just as his role as the duke of Vienna influences and problematizes each of the confessions that he takes as a friar, so his role as a friar seems to have some influence on the confession that he hears as a ruler. Angelo wishes his confession to be a legal confession, complete with a sentence that he believes to be appropriate to his crime. The duke then inverts the confession, stripping it of its legal nature and turning it into a plea for forgiveness and absolution. The final scene represents a strange conflation of both heavenly and earthly justice, answering Angelo's confession with a pardon that he does not want, and answering Isabella's chaste virtue with a marriage proposal to which she does not respond. Blending his twin roles of father confessor and tolerant ruler, the duke dominates the final scene, imposing forgiveness and restoring order to a divided city. Slippery definitions of sin and virtue and fluid interpretations of strict laws come to characterize both the duke and the play itself, and the city of Vienna ends the play in a harmony that is nearly as problematic as the disorder that began the play.

Both *Hamlet* and *Measure for Measure* represent the conflict between two extreme ideals of justice, each one impossible to attain. Through religious and legal confessions, the characters explore not only the consequences of sin but its very nature as they debate intention, action, and the relative merits of mercy and contrition in an effort to arrive at a form of justice that is equal parts sacred and secular. Through Angelo and Claudius, audiences experience the distance between legal and religious authority, while characters such as the duke and Hamlet attempt to serve both ends simultaneously. The confusion and frustration of the ritual in both plays asks audiences to consider the nature of absolution and the agents who administer it.

Notes

1. A. C. Crawley, ed., *Everyman*, University of Michigan Digital Library, accessed May 1, 2012, http://quod.lib.umich.edu/c/cme/Everyman/1:11?rgn=div1;view=fulltext (scene 12, lines 617–18).

2. David N. Beauregard, *Catholic Theology in Shakespeare's Plays* (Cranbury, NJ: Rosemont Publishing, 2008), 29.

3. Tracey Sowerby, *Renaissance and Reform in Tudor England: The Careers of Sir Richard Morison c. 1513–1556* (New York: Oxford University Press, 2010), 162.

4. Beauregard, *Catholic Theology*, 29.

5. William Shakespeare, *Hamlet*, ed. A. R. Braunmuller (New York: Penguin, 2001), 3.3.36.

6. Ibid., 1.4.90.

7. Ibid., 3.3.51–55.

8. Ibid., 3.3.97–98.

9. Ibid., 3.3.57–64.

10. Ibid., 3.3.76–79.

11. Romans 1:29–32.

12. William Shakespeare, *Measure for Measure*, ed. J. W. Lever (London: Arden, 1994), 2.2.37.

13. Ibid., 2.2.71,73.

14. Ibid., 2.2.90–100.

15. Ibid., 2.2.137–39.

16. Ibid., 1.3.12.

17. Randall R. Curren, *A Companion to the Philosophy of Education* (Oxford: Blackwell, 2003), 58.

18. Shakespeare, *Measure for Measure*, 2.4.158–60.

19. Curren, *Companion*, 58.

20. Anthony Kenny, *A Brief History of Western Philosophy* (Oxford: Blackwell, 1998), 147.

21. Shakespeare, *Hamlet*, 3.3.97.

22. Shakespeare, *Measure for Measure*, 2.4.2–4.

23. Shakespeare, *Hamlet*, 3.3.38–40.

24. Shakespeare, *Measure for Measure*, 2.4.4–7.

25. Ibid., 2.4.5.

26. Elizabeth Hansen, *Discovering the Subject in Renaissance England* (Cambridge: Cambridge University Press, 1998), 67.

27. Ibid.

28. Shakespeare, *Measure for Measure*, 2.3.21–24.

29. Hansen, *Discovering the Subject*, 67.

30. Ibid.

31. Shakespeare, *Measure for Measure*, 4.3.22, 47, 50–51.

32. Ibid., 4.3.53–55.

33. Hansen, *Discovering the Subject*, 67.

34. Shakespeare, *Measure for Measure*, 5.1.449–51.

35. Ibid., 5.451–52.

36. Saint Augustine of Hippo, *On the Trinity: 8–15* (Cambridge; Cambridge University Press, 2002), 96.

37. Peter Abelard, *Ethics*, excerpt in Andrew Schoedinger, *Readings in Medieval Philosophy* (New York: Oxford University Press, 1996), 129.

38. Curren, *Companion*, 58.

39. Ibid.

40. John Marenbon, *Early Medieval Philosophy (480–1150): An Introduction* (London, Routledge, 1983), 165.

41. Shakespeare, *Measure for Measure*, 5.1.364–72.

42. Derek Cohen, *The Politics of Shakespeare* (London: MacMillan, 1993), 121.

Treasure in Clay Jars

Christian Liturgical Drama in Theory and Praxis

Charles A. Gillespie, Justin Kosec, and Kate Stratton

O VER THE course of the 2011–2012 academic year, the authors began to develop a form of liturgical drama for the context of Christian worship that combines humor, "reverent irreverence," confessional storytelling, intentionally Christian theology and biblical study, and contemporary theatre technique. In collaboration with Maggi Dawn, the dean of chapel at Yale Divinity School (YDS), and the chapel staff, we continue to produce dramas anchored to the liturgical setting that engage the lived experience of the community and the scriptures.

In this essay we will reflect on the early days of this experiment in worship art: the development of a rehearsal methodology that arises out of the combination of Christian community and theatrical technique. Then, addressing questions of ritual function and the ways actors represent communities, we will explore its theoretical underpinnings. Lastly, we will consider one possible transformative impact on the worship community: the power of an embodied, multivocal liturgical drama to foster a greater sense of *communitas*.

The Methodology of Liturgical Drama: A Case Study

Our liturgical drama project arose from the particular context of Yale Divinity School. While YDS admits students from a variety of religious backgrounds, the institution intentionally maintains a progressive Christian culture. At the heart of the community's worship life lies Marquand Chapel, which offers ecumenical (interdenominationally Christian) services each morning. Most Marquand Chapel services are assigned to a student liturgist, who then coordinates the details of the service with the preacher, musicians, and the chapel leadership staff. The seeds of our liturgical drama project took root over the course of a few days in September 2011, when members of the Marquand Chapel ministry team asked us to perform a brief improvisational drama in conversation with a student sermon. We were chosen because of our previous experience in drama (both academically and professionally) and our work in a YDS student theatre troupe. Additionally, we had performed a short prewritten scene as part of an Easter service the previous year. This time, we were charged with preparing a framework for an improvised scene based on the day's scripture and performing it during worship as a lead-in to a student preacher's senior sermon. The sermon, we were told, would explicate 2 Corinthians 4:7: "But we have this treasure in clay jars, so that it may be made clear that this extraordinary power belongs to God and does not come from us."[1]

With no more direction than this, we met to develop and rehearse our drama. We began with a collective exegetical study of 2 Corinthians 4, reading and discussing the chapter to find some way to dramatize it. This passage lacked a strong narrative thread, however, which made it difficult to translate into a scene. Further, and perhaps more worrisome, we felt a pressure to perform well, and we allowed this to sideline any commitment to an honest embodiment of a scriptural interpretation. We believed our drama could bear real liturgical potential, yet we worried that some congregants would not accept improvisational theatre as a "legitimate" mode of worship. We were anxious to win "converts," so to speak, with an exceptional scene. And what, did we think, would make a good scene? We clung to a few standard improvisational strictures to guide us and additionally assumed our scene must (1) draw its particularities from community life; (2) include audience/congregation involvement, in the form of suggestions; (3) have a clear beginning, middle, and end; and (4) be funny.

Striving to adhere to these guidelines, we settled on a preliminary framework for our improvisation. It would be set during coffee hour, a period of fellowship and refreshment that immediately follows Marquand Chapel services each morning. At the scene's opening, three characters would converge on the last cup of coffee, squabbling briefly over it. Each would argue that he or she deserved it based on the number of urgent tasks (e.g., school assignments, work, internship requirements) each needed to complete that day. These "tasks" would not be products of our own imaginations, however, but would come from the congregation: at the start of the service, the worshippers would be invited to detail actual stressors weighing on them that day and deposit them into a clay jar—a material nod to the content of the biblical passage—for use by the performers during the scene.

In the middle of the scene, one of us would shift from claiming the coffee for him or herself to insisting another take it. The remaining characters would experience this shift in succession until one character would "win" the drink. The scene would end with a final "button," a joke with which the victor would reveal a secret distaste for coffee.

We had achieved a scene that made sense at the time. Yet as we spoke with the preacher during rehearsal the following evening, it quickly became clear that our interpretation of 2 Corinthians 4 jarred badly with the message the preacher intended to offer. There was no reconciling the two. Furthermore, the absurdity and arbitrariness of our scene's driving conflict (procurement of coffee) and our own caricatured responses in the drama—both of which would likely have suited the tone and style of a "secular" improv show—felt out of place within the liturgical context. Where had we gone wrong? We had privileged the potential entertainment value of our scene, an impulse fueled by our own desire to perform well and be well received, over the potential for the scene's liturgical efficacy.

In *Liberating Rites: Understanding the Transformative Power of Ritual*, Tom F. Driver makes a distinction between performance and transformance: "*To do* something while *displaying* the doing equals *performance*," he explains, but "a ritual is '*transformance*'—a performance designed to change a situation." Furthermore, Driver delineates between the essence and execution of art and ritual: "Art is *play* done workfully, but ritual is *work* done playfully." Without our intending to do so, our original scene, if performed in worship, would have injected a moment of superfluous art into ritual. We had cultivated the scene without fully considering the different needs and means required by its ritual context. Thus, the scene was at its heart playful, but it did not transport. It did not serve a purpose. In worship it would have proven sensational—it would, in Driver's words, have been able to "bear no witness at all." We were trying to execute a performance in worship, when what we had hoped for was a "transformance."[2]

In the rehearsal with our preacher and our liturgist, we knew instantly we had to throw out our previous night's work. But then, where to begin? How could we move from entertainment to efficacy? How could we transmute our performative scene into a transformative one? By the end of the night, we had a scene that worked. It arose through (1) careful attention to the message of the source text (2 Corinthians 4); (2) honest, vulnerable conversation; and (3) a realization of how our scene functioned liturgically.

We started to rework our drama with a simple question: What does the preacher intend to preach? We asked him to explain his interpretation of 2 Corinthians 4. He hoped to communicate that we are all are cracked clay jars filled with inadequacies, unresolved conflicts, and emotional anxieties. But this does not keep God from using us; in fact, we cracked-clay-jar people are precisely the sort of people God chooses to use.

Once we understood the preacher's sermon, we attempted to represent his theme dramatically. This time, instead of constructing a humorous drama tangentially related to 2 Corinthians 4, we wanted to focus our drama on the meaning of the biblical text by using embodied performance as a true-to-life manifestation of the preacher's message. And we intended to bring it to life within the actual context and common social dramas experienced by the YDS community.

With an idea of what the scene should accomplish, but no clear sense of *how*, we took a step back. What did it mean for the YDS community to be a community filled with "clay jar" people? Before we could answer that question for the community, we had to answer it for ourselves. So we set aside pressure to create a finished product, ignoring the fact that our chapel service would take place, whether we were ready or not, the following morning. We took our time and allowed our conversation to wander. We shared our own stories with one another: What brought us to YDS? What did we hope to do with our degrees? What did "ministry" mean to us? And how did our hopes and expectations for divinity school cohere with or depart from the reality of our Yale experience?

In *A Feminist Ethic of Risk*, Sharon Welch argues that the goal of communicative ethics—a "mutually self-critical engagement with difference" in which participants work *with* and not *for* others—is "community and solidarity." Community and solidarity cannot be achieved, however, without transformative communication, the three guidelines of which Welch borrows from Garth Baker-Fletcher: (1) genuine interest, (2) genuine nonvolatile confrontation, and (3) genuine perseverance.[3] By chance, our rehearsal conversation followed these guidelines, as we listened to one another's stories, asked curious probing questions, and gently challenged one another's assumptions.

Our conversation was personal, vulnerable, and honest. It was raw confession, insofar as we shared details and anxieties we might have hidden in any other situation at YDS. Several themes emerged: (1) each of us came to YDS wanting, somehow, to cultivate tools that would help to heal the Church, the academy, our local communities, or even the wider world; (2) none of us felt truly up to these tasks; and (3) we felt mired in our own shortcomings or in the limitations of the academy. Some of us carried a daily sense of our own inadequacy: a fear that our inability to perform in classes suggested that we could never perform our vocations. Some of us struggled with an unsettling lack of passion: we excelled in schoolwork yet felt apathetic about it, leading us to wonder if we were on the right vocational path. And some of us doubted the utility of our curriculum: we had clear vocational goals but questioned whether our classroom work was preparing us for the future. As we shared, it became clear that our stories were concrete, lived expressions of 2 Corinthians 4. They were illustrative of the human experiences of vulnerability, finitude, and fallibility—of feeling like a "clay jar" in a world of "treasure."

Furthermore, we recalled similar conversations with other members of our community; we knew we were not the only ones with such struggles. We discovered, in this moment of sharing, a phenomenon Driver notes in *Liberating Rites*: "In the confessional mode, selfhood is both personal and communal."[4] Key to this confessional mode is truth telling; and by telling the truth about ourselves, we had discovered truths about our community.

Our scene finally and organically arose from this conversation. We would, through drama, give voice to our own—and by extension, our fellow worshippers'—"clay jar" experiences. We set the scene after a community meal as three new friends awaited the arrival of a university shuttle, prime time for an end-of-week honest conversation. One character struggled with inadequacy, another with lack of passion, and the third with doubt about his course of study. We still planned to draw congregation-generated suggestions from a clay jar. These suggestions would combine with our rehearsal conversation to create the meat of the scene: the embodied, communal interpretation of the preacher's homiletic argument.

At this point, we had two of the three ingredients for a transformative moment of liturgical drama: first, careful engagement with a biblical text; and second, honest and vulnerable (confessional) conversation. We tried the new scene a few times; it still wasn't working. Though the scene felt authentic—it represented each person in the room and many we knew outside the room as well—there was something about its structure that overrode the message. We had not yet developed a sense of the scene's function within the liturgy, the third crucial ingredient.

Such sensitivity demands careful balance, for there are many considerations that may shape any given worship service. One should determine what a drama should accomplish and allow this desired liturgical function to shape its structure. Will the drama provide a word of welcome, or a sending, or an exegetical reflection on the text? One must also craft a drama's content with sensitivity to its contribution to the whole liturgy. How does the message of the drama need to connect to the scripture read in worship? How does it interface with the message of the preacher? What emotional tone does the piece need to strike? How will this tone affect the emotional arc of worship? Worship planning may also place logistical demands on a drama: How much time does a drama have to unfold? The flow of time beyond an individual worship service also affects the content of a drama. Where does a particular worship service fall on the liturgical calendar? What current events are important to the gathered community? For example, a series of Holy Week dramas might move from celebratory (Palm Sunday) to somber (Good Friday). A single Easter service could call for dramas that strike any number of emotions: celebration, fear, confusion, and so forth. Defining the drama's liturgical function becomes a rubric for making theatrical choices. A drama intending to welcome would utilize humor in a very different way from a drama meant to create space for meditation on a painful topic.

In the case of "Treasure in Clay Jars," we had not yet allowed for the drama's liturgical function to help shape its form. Within its liturgical context, our scene was meant to lead into the preacher's sermon, to set it up by introducing the vulnerability, insecurity, and challenges of day-to-day life faced by every member of the gathered community. It was supposed to present a guiding problem, but we had been trying to find a way to include a theological solution. We had been searching for an ending, but we realized that we did not need any sort of "button" at all. We did not need to solve our characters' struggles neatly; instead, we could leave the scene hanging on an unsatisfactory question: "So what do we *do* about this (clay jar experience)?" And we would not attempt an answer.

The next day, in worship, congregants deposited their current stressors into the clay jar. We worshipped with the congregation, leaving our seats only when it was our time to perform. As we began our scene, the energy in Marquand Chapel shifted. Laughter erupted—a laughter of recognition—as we drew congregants' suggestions and named them as our own. When our characters asked one another, "So what do we *do* about this," the question hung in the air, uneasy, unresolved. A reverential silence fell. As we sat down and the preacher took the floor, we felt that something in the room had changed. Our drama had become what we had originally intended it to be, though we did not have the language for it at the time: a transformation, a "performance designed to change a situation."[5]

Early in our planning, we were concerned about how our scene might be perceived by the worshipping congregation. In the end, we found a rather paradoxical solution: we set aside our desire to make a "good, complete" scene. In worship, a theatrical moment fails if it serves as an entertaining break from the "real liturgy." Liturgical drama may lose all its effectiveness when congregants step into the role of theatre critics or consumers—those present to watch a "performance" that occurs separate from the flow of worship.

That feeling of separation between the liturgy and the drama can be a symptom of "modularity": the sense that discrete moments of liturgical action might be swapped in and out as interchangeable parts.[6] Our work takes strides to avoid modularity by consciously attending to the liturgical context of the drama. Liturgy does not stop so that theatre can begin. The two must endeavor to work together, in much the same way that spoken prayers and readings reinterpret and subtly transition to sung hymns or preached sermons. A liturgy that avoids modularity considers each aspect to be part of an integrated whole, and to remove any one aspect would have a significant impact on the efficacy of the worship service. When considered in liturgical context, a drama avoids modularity through its lack of a traditional theatrical ending.[7] This was not simply a solution for the "Treasure in Clay Jars" scene: it is foundational to our practice. Our dramas rarely "resolve" their plots; questions remain open with many possible answers. Scenes may end, but they often resist offering a neat conclusion, a final button-joke, or a moment of "curtain call" complete with bows. This helps emphasize that the drama belongs to the greater liturgy.

Since this initial effort, we have further refined our methodology; now, we follow a rigorous rehearsal process that includes an organic and shifting combination of group biblical exegesis, consideration for liturgical function, and vulnerability-sharing conversation. This methodology of contextualized rehearsal is what defines our practice of liturgical drama.

Each of these three dimensions—a hermeneutic for biblical exegesis in the community, drama within the context of Christian liturgy, and community-building conversation—is crucial and deserves further examination. For the purpose of this study, we will focus the remainder of our efforts on the contribution of one of these dimensions. We believe liturgical drama that arises out of the community has the greatest capacity to be a transformance when the people involved—actors, liturgists, congregations—gather together in open, confessional conversation. What is the importance of conversation to community building? And how does the confessional mode of a rehearsal conversation come to embody the experience of a worshipping community?

Seeds of Transformance:
Conversation, Rehearsal, and Polysemy

As we have suggested, the success of our liturgical dramas hinges, perhaps above all, on one particular exercise: careful cultivation of intentionally pressure-free rehearsals where transformative, confessional conversations may arise. Conversation becomes not just part of rehearsal, but its center. In "Towards a Poetics of Performance," Richard Schechner describes a similar experience in the inchoate, coalescing process of rehearsal at The Performance Group. In their early phase, such rehearsals are "jerky and disjointed, often incoherent." Artists involved in the process—actors, directors, designers—provide input but with little overall clarity of vision; instead, they seek a vision that will arise in their midst: "The work is indeed a hunt, actions with 'high information potential' but very little goal-orientation. Even in working on texted material this kind of 'looking around' marks early rehearsals: actors try a variety of interpretations, designers bring in many sketches and models most of which are rejected, the director doesn't really know what he wants."[8] All this initial "looking around" is a quest for some kind of collaborative message. The structured work of the rehearsal, which involves "repetition, simplification, exaggeration, rhythmic action, the transformation of 'natural sequences' of behavior into 'composed sequences,'" mimics the structured work of ritual preparation. This leads Schechner to claim that "the essential ritual action of theatre takes place during rehearsals"—that is, rehearsals are the theatrical location of the repetitive, rhythmic, composed sequences that frequently define ritual.[9]

Centering our rehearsal methodology on conversation broadens the definition of rehearsal itself. Rehearsal occurs whenever and wherever such conversations take place: in the initial planning and brainstorming sessions that determine the shape of a service; during collaborative exegetical work; within personal conversations that are then interpreted into a script and reshaped by actors as they practice. Each period of preparation for a liturgical drama, each formal or informal "rehearsal" conversation, creates the space for the theological artists involved—the preacher, the musical director, the dramatists, the liturgists—to allow their minds to range freely over the material at hand, including biblical texts, events in the life of the community, and the timing of the liturgical year.

By the time actors are preparing for the actual worship service, they are blending their own rhythms and their own experiences with those contained within the "script" (textual or improvised)—a script that has been generated through the effort of the larger community. As they practice their lines and embody this script, they rehearse this larger "rehearsal" of the community, further contributing to the development of the scene's creative content by their participation as embodied performers.[10]

When the script is finally executed in worship, it is impossible to say who the actor represents. Does he reveal his own fears or disappointments or joys, those of the wider community, the scriptwriter (if there is one), the liturgist, the biblical author, a close friend, a stranger? When the liturgical drama is successful, these are all layers of its representation. But in the moment of worship it includes an additional layer: the actor becomes a metaphorical representation of those present in worship as well. The drama represents a corporate emotional landscape. Each character is polysemous, representing multiple layers of meaning bundled together.

Polysemous meaning arises by virtue of the embodied nature of the dramatic art form. In *Metaphor and Material Culture*, Christopher Tilley writes, "The body is the ground or anchor by means of which we locate ourselves in the world, perceive and apprehend it." The body is a site of a multiplicitous meaning making: "Structures of bodily experience work their way up into abstract meanings, embodied imagination. The body, culture, and metaphor act so as to constitute each other."[11] As they enact a script that itself bears the load of a multiplicity of meanings, actors in the liturgical drama work their way into abstract meanings; they become the embodied imagination of the worshippers. They are thus freed to explore spirituality, engage the Bible, and question the community experience as metaphorical representatives of the gathered body of worshippers. They are inherently polysemous. "Underlying both verbal and solid metaphor is polysemy. The polysemy of words and the polysemous condensation of meanings in things both permit metaphorical elaboration."[12] In a linguistic metaphor, such polysemy arises out of the strata of meanings in words themselves. As embodied metaphors, the actors in a liturgical drama become polysemous performers who condense a series of meanings on behalf of the worshippers. They condense sites of textual meaning (exegesis) and theological meaning through the culturally mediated forms of their own bodies: their own natural speech patterns, their own physical presence and gesticulation, their own performative self-disclosure.

It is crucial that this embodiment occur in the ritual space of Christian worship. As embodied imaginations, actors in the liturgical drama fulfill something of Nicole Boivin's image for how the material (here, the embodied actor) can explicate the mysterious, the difficult, the ineffable: "Ritual activity and material culture are able to evoke such comparisons at a deeper and more physical level that seems to enable elusive concepts to be understood, and cosmological belief systems to be felt rather than just understood."[13] Concepts that might otherwise remain heady and distant (e.g., theological notions of God's relationship to humanity, a difficult or confusing biblical text, etc.) may become relatable and accessible through the actors' bodily storytelling. But far more than simply explaining theology or biblical hermeneutics, as the worshipping community's embodied imagination, the actors in a liturgical drama empower the congregation to become cocreators of these ideas. These come into being in the very midst of the congregation, because "ideas and cultural understandings do not precede, but rather are helped into becoming by, the material world and human engagement with it during the course of ritual activity."[14] The liturgical drama, as a polysemous focal point of worship, opens the congregation to a range of meaning making.

In this way a liturgical drama is not dissimilar to Don M. Wardlaw's concept of good preaching, which he describes as a vortex: "As the Word springs forth from the vortex of its ancient setting to express itself through the vortex of text/preacher/people in social context, the Word of God *happens*; it becomes a proclamation even in the lives of the people experiencing the sermon."[15] The preacher delivers the Word of God to the people and from the midst of the people, and their collective imaginations create some new sense out of the words of the preacher that generates meaning for the entire community. But we argue that meaning making and efficacy in liturgical drama arise out of a different admixture of elements. Rather than a text/preacher/people dynamic, effective liturgical drama functions instead like concentric vortices: the vortex created by the text/dramatic script/actors is nestled inside the vortex created by the text/liturgical script/people. They are representative of one another and constitutive of one another. And when the liturgical drama is performed within this mutually constitutive vortex, it transmutes performance into transformance (see figure 1).

Let us return for a moment to consider the original rehearsal process, the foundational and generative moments when the actors, the dramatic script, and the biblical text intersect and begin to cohere. These early rehearsals gather ritual quality and power, becoming themselves acts of worship that will enliven and generate the later act of corporate worship. In the worship event, liturgical drama is not a finished product to be consumed by a passive audience; rather, it continues the ranging and creative openness to new discoveries characteristic of Schechner's rehearsal process. As actors step up to perform their script they are in essence inviting the congregation to rehearse with them one particular performance of Christian living. They become worship leaders who step forth from the congregation to embody its imaginative struggle with the biblical text, represented as their own continued, polysemous "rehearsal" of the liturgical drama.

The foundation of this ongoing "rehearsal" is, as we have already discussed, vulnerable conversation, held in the confessional mode during the

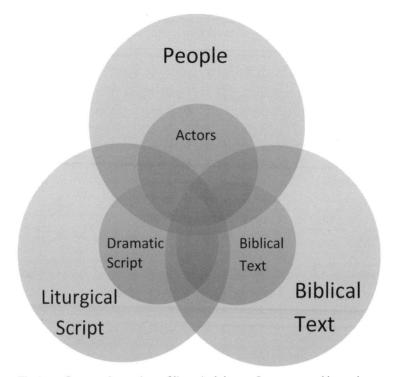

Figure 1. Concentric vortices of liturgical drama. Image created by authors.

rehearsal process. This confessional mode itself has a ritual quality: "The confession finds, or perhaps makes, its community."[16] The actors can only serve as the embodied imagination of the worshippers when they engage in a truth telling on behalf of that community, and when the truth they tell arises out of that community. In that moment, when they perform confession for themselves and for others, "the situation of the individual comes to be seen as something the community shares, and the community is legitimated as the necessary complement of the individual."[17] One of liturgical drama's many potential fruits is the cultivation of community.

Toward a Conclusion: Making Space
for Transformation within Community

In the ritual moment, the community invites performers of a liturgical drama to step into the confessional mode on their behalf. Liturgical drama thus facilitates the fuller participation of the entire assembly—

and a greater sense of communitas—by professing the silent, the hidden, and the unspoken through dramatic presentation. Liturgical drama thus becomes a communal, cataphatic experience of an individual, apophatic experience. It permits community to speak truthfully to itself. The actors in a liturgical drama become the embodied imagination and lived experience of the assembly, thereby gathering the entire assembly into an ongoing, creative process of rehearsal. There, the voices of all are free from the critical, evaluative, self- or community-imposed expectations of a "proper" performance. This, finally, is one of the hopes of our liturgical drama: to create plain old acceptance in worship, and for this acceptance to arise out of confessional conversation.

But our methodology does not ultimately seek to *create* such moments of transformative experience. Transformance cannot be an end to which one aspires, nor something created solely because one wants it. Transformance arises in the midst of a community that makes space for it. Furthermore, each community has different standards for, or even vocabularies of, what counts as a transformative experience. We do not strive to make universal prescriptions for liturgical drama, or to reduce the art to measurable outcomes (such as "achieving transformance"). Instead, we want to present our own creative methodology: driven by context for the sake of one particular gathered community, guided by vulnerable and honest communication, and rooted in engagement with our scriptures and inherited tradition. Each drama grows out of an openness to discovery. It is this openness—not dedication to artistic form, or to the centrality of script or playwright or ensemble, or a commitment to prescribed outcomes, or the desire for a perfectly "finished" product—that is at the heart of our practice.

Such adaptable openness is also what makes liturgical drama broadly transferable. While this artistic approach germinated in YDS's Marquand Chapel, a commitment to context opens the form for use in a variety of other circumstances and spaces (perhaps even to "secular" gatherings outside of plainly Christian worship). In each case, the very content of a transformative scene will come from the community itself as its members relate firsthand their fears, hopes, disappointments, and dreams. And indeed this is what we have experienced with liturgical dramas as we have practiced them in other Christian congregations (such as Mayfield Salisbury Parish Church in Edinburgh, Scotland, and also in a recontextualized version of the "Treasure in Clay Jars" scene executed at the SETC Theatre Symposium).[18]

As an interdisciplinary practice, liturgical drama builds bridges between many fields and introduces strange academic bedfellows (liturgical theology and material culture studies; communicative ethics and performance studies; pastoral care and applied theatre; etc.). Theatre, ritual, and religion are all resources for this conversation; much more can be said to deepen the connections between them. We have labored to show that a liturgical drama may avoid easy answers and foregone conclusions, preferring instead to raise questions, challenge assumptions, and create the conditions for transformative change to occur. Liturgical drama as we practice it is still in development—but it will always be, for such drama must grow from and nimbly respond to the needs of its community. In crafting any semblance of transformation, we must seek not only artistic integrity or fidelity to our community's scripture, but also the simple truth of who we are as individuals, and claim—perhaps boldly, perhaps with whatever halting courage we can muster—who we are in relationship to one another.

Notes

1. Holy Bible, NRSV, New Revised Standard Version (New York: Harper Bibles, 2007).
2. Tom F. Driver, *Liberating Rites: Understanding the Transformative Power of Ritual* (Boulder, CO: Westview, 1998), 212.
3. Sharon D. Welch, *A Feminist Ethic of Risk* (Minneapolis: Fortress, 1990), 15–16.
4. Driver, *Liberating Rites*, 118.
5. Ibid., 212.
6. Ronald L. Grimes, in conversation with the authors, January 26, 2012.
7. When explicating the importance of unity in *Poetics*, Aristotle says a piece of art "must represent one action, a complete whole, with its several incidents so closely connected that the transposal or withdrawal of any one of them will disjoin and dislocate the whole. For that which makes no perceptible difference by its presence or absence is no real part of the whole"; *Philosophies of Art and Beauty*, ed. Albert Hofstadter and Richard Kuhns (Chicago: University of Chicago Press, 1976), 106. Similarly, foundational liturgical theologian Alexander Schmemann explains that the liturgy "is a whole, within which everything, the words of prayer, lections, chanting, ceremonies, the relationship of all these things in a 'sequence' or 'order' only all this together defines the meaning of the whole and is therefore the proper subject of study and theological evaluation"; *Introduction to Liturgical Theology*, trans. Asheleigh Moorehouse (New York: St Vladimir's Seminary Press, 2003), 19. Note, though, that "unity" in Aristotle implies a completed action with a clearly defined beginning, middle, and end. In practice our liturgical dramas frequently avoid such internal completion, relying instead on the liturgical structure to suggest openings or conclusions.
8. Richard Schechner, "Towards a Poetics of Performance," in *Essays on Performance Theory, 1970–1976* (New York: Drama Book Specialists, 1977), 135.
9. Ibid., 136, 133.

10. We often embrace this as an artistic and aesthetic choice: even when actors have a script memorized we hold scripts in hand during the worship event.

11. Christopher Y. Tilley, *Metaphor and Material Culture* (Malden, MA: Blackwell, 2000), 34–35.

12. Christopher Y. Tilley, *Material Culture and the Text: The Art of Ambiguity* (London: Routledge, 1991), 263.

13. Nicole Boivin, "Grasping the Elusive and Unknowable: Material Culture in Ritual Practice," *Material Religion: The Journal of Objects, Art and Belief* 5, no. 3 (2009): 263–64.

14. Ibid., 274.

15. Don M. Wardlaw, "Preaching as the Interface of Two Social Worlds," in *Preaching as a Social Act: Theology and Practice*, ed. Arthur Van Seters (Nashville: Abingdon, 1988), 78.

16. Driver, *Liberating Rites*, 118.

17. Ibid.

18. At the symposium, we presented a version of the "Treasure in Clay Jars" scene specially adapted for the conference. Our framing question was, "What has been challenging you these past few days (i.e. something about the conference, something from home, travel challenges, social awkwardness, etc.)?" Using the responses we received, as well as characters we developed who broadly embodied the disciplines at the conference (ritual studies, theatre, religion), we performed a recontextualized "clay jar" improvisation. At Mayfield Salisbury we followed our methodology to produce a different scene, which we tailored to that specific congregation in coordination with Reverend Scott McKenna. For a write-up of our visit to Mayfield Salisbury, see: http://www.mayfieldsalisbury.org/news/news-info.asp?NewsID=66.

Between Piety and Sacrilege

Muslim Theatre and Performance

Thomas King

ICONOCLASTIC impulses among Muslims are supposed to have prevented the development of Muslim theatre and performance prior to the introduction of European theatrical styles and architecture in the late nineteenth and early twentieth centuries. In fact, the second of the commandments that Moses brought down from Mount Sinai is much more explicit in its prohibition of representation than anything in the Koran. The Koran prohibits idolatry but not "graven images." Implicitly, though, if idolatry is prohibited, then the making of idols for the idolaters to worship is also prohibited. Moreover, there are hadith that can be interpreted to mean that representation is forbidden.[1] Nevertheless, in spite of any reservations about representation leading to idolatry, there is a rich performance and theatre tradition in Muslim lands that predates the introduction of Western styles and influences. Some performances are even staged where both actors and audience believe that they are demonstrating Muslim religious fervor and piety by their participation. All performances, even those performances most firmly rooted in Muslim rites and ceremonies, seem to originate in pre-Islamic rituals and observances.[2]

The Iranian *ta'ziyeh* play is one of the most elaborate instances of Muslim performance. Though it is performed in the service of Iranian, Muslim, Shi'ite worship, theological arguments to defend it against charges of idolatry have been advanced.

Shi'ites believe that Ali, the son-in-law and cousin of Muhammad, should have been chosen as the leader of the Muslim community after Muhammad's death. He was passed over three times, and when he finally became the fourth caliph, he was assassinated. Shi'ites who hoped to restore the caliphate to the descendants of Muhammad invited Hussein, the son of Ali and the grandson of Muhammad, to join them at Kufa, about one hundred miles south of Baghdad. On his way to Kufa, Hussein and his followers and family were attacked and massacred at Karbala on the tenth of the Muslim month of Ashura (formerly known as Muharram). In Iran, Ashura is commemorated by the staging of ta'ziyeh plays reenacting the battle of Karbala and events leading up to and following it. The actors in these plays represent not just human beings, but members of the Prophet's family.

Given the traditional Muslim animus against representation, ta'ziyeh in Iran has inspired arguments to legitimate its performance. These are usually based on the principle of "imitation," which comes from a hadith that states: "Whoever makes himself resemble a group is in the category of that group." That is, if one imitates the good, then one is in the category of the good.[3] The actors who imitate Hussein and his party are making themselves resemble "the good" (in this case, members of the Prophet's family). Even given the reassurance of the hadith on imitation, however, ta'ziyeh actors are sometimes said to be "carrying" a role rather than representing a human being. In the past, actors who knew their parts nonetheless held scripts, and the director sometimes joined the actors onstage to visibly instruct and assist them. The influence of Western acting styles has all but ended script carrying, but at the Lincoln Center performance in 2002, actors who were ready to sing or to speak ostentatiously cued the musicians to play or stop playing even though the musicians had no part in the historical event the actors were staging (see figure 1).[4]

Actors playing the villains who massacre Hussein and his family are in a particularly difficult position. According to the hadith about imitation, they are making themselves resemble the oppressors of the Shi'ites and putting themselves in the category of the bad. To escape this dilemma, they "act with tears in their eyes, or use asides commenting on the cruelty of the character they portray."[5] Iraj Anvar says that the "performer who played the part of a villain would curse and discredit the character he played, announcing that he was just playing a part."[6]

The audience may benefit from resembling the good as much as the actors. When spectators feel the sorrow that Hussein and his companions felt, they resemble the martyrs at Karbala and join the actors in the category of the good. When actors in the ta'ziyeh weep and beat their chests, audiences join them.[7] Some Muslim theologians say that anyone who weeps for himself and causes others to weep is one of the good.[8] Many Muslims see the ta'ziyeh as a means to salvation: "Anyone who cries for Hussein or causes someone to cry for Hussein shall go directly to paradise."[9]

Most scholars agree that the ta'ziyeh plays originated in nontheatrical ritual performances commemorating the battle of Karbala.[10] Some believe these ceremonies are themselves rooted in pre-Islamic rituals of mourn-

Figure 1. Shemr, supported by two enemy soldiers, reads his lines. Tehran, Iran, 2004. Photograph by Khanum Tajik; courtesy of Reza Khaki; from the collection of Peter J. Chelkowski.

ing for dead heroes.[11] The word *ta'ziyeh* means "mourning" or "condolence" and includes a whole range of Muharram activities and observances. Before the plays existed, there were public recitations describing the battle and processions of mourners in the streets beating themselves with chains or striking their heads with sharp objects to cover themselves with blood. Vehicles carried living tableaux representing the massacred family of Hussein. At some point, probably during the Christian eighteenth century, the tableaux began to speak and became plays. Public recitations and processions of mourners flagellating and bleeding, however, have remained a part of Muharram activities (see figure 2).

The theological arguments enabling ta'ziyeh plays in Iran have not been persuasive in other parts of the Shi'ite community. Shi'ites in Pakistan, who have roots in Iran and mourn the death of the imam Hussein with recitations and processions, do not perform plays. According to Muhammad Ja'far Mahjub, "Even the Shi'ites living as minorities in non-Shi'a countries view these performances with astonishment. When an experienced Pakistani director and actor, who had worked for years in large and reputable theatres in England, witnessed the *ta'ziyeh* at the Shiraz Festival of Arts; he remarked . . . , 'I was struck by seeing this performance! It is really very remarkable that the people of Iran . . . permit someone to play the roles of the Imams and sacred figures of the faith.'"[12]

Figure 2. A modernized float on a flatbed truck is a mobile stage for a Karbala scene in this processional *ta'ziyeh*. Mehriz, Iran, 1996. Courtesy of J. Ghazbanpour, from the collection of Peter J. Chelkowski.

In India, the term *ta'ziyeh* does not refer to a play, but to a replica of Hussein's tomb that is carried in procession and then buried.[13]

The divide between Sunni and Shi'a is political as well as religious, and this division has been manifest in the ta'ziyeh activities staged in observance of Muharram and Ashura. Shi'ism is a religion of outsiders. Its founding heroes were deprived of what Shi'ites believe was their rightful place in the community of Muslims and killed.[14] Sunnis in Morocco do not mourn during Muharram; they celebrate victory.[15] The Islamic revolution of the 1970s in Iran appropriated ta'ziyeh for its purposes and characterized the shah as Yazid, the caliph who ordered the massacre at Karbala. In the war with Iraq in the 1980s, Saddam Hussein became Yazid and Iranian youths were called to become martyrs like those at Karbala. Muharram observances have broken into open combat between Sunnis and Shi'ites, with violence analogous to that between Protestants and Catholics during the parade season in Northern Ireland. As Mayel Baktash writes:

> The mourning ceremonies of the Buyid period had an immediate external objective: opposition to the power and establishment of the Sunnis. . . . The mourners were confronted with a reaction on the part of the Baghdad Sunnis, and riots ensued.

On Ashura 363 A.H./A.D. 973 the Sunnis brought out a procession to commemorate the Battle of the Camel. . . . They said that they were going to fight the supporters of Ali. When the processions of the two factions met each other, fighting erupted. The famous bloody riots in the Karkh quarter of Baghdad continued until after the Buyid period.[16]

Ta'ziyeh is an example of Muslim performance which, though it may be used politically, is fully integrated into Muslim worship. Nevertheless, some have felt the need to defend the plays with theological justifications against any taint of idolatry. Moreover, even instances of ceremonies in commemoration of Ashura that do not include plays still represent the massacred family of Hussein in living tableaux and in recitations describing the battle of Karbala or in replicas of Hussein's tomb. Paradoxically, the performances celebrate Islam and Shi'ism in a form that probably has roots in pagan ritual and invites worshippers to respond to representations in ways that could be interpreted as idolatry.

Forms of Muslim performance that are not directly connected to any religious observance or ritual were prevalent in the Ottoman Empire. Storytellers called *meddahs* told mostly comic stories that emphasized dialogue in which the meddah imitated multiple voices and characters.[17] Turkish *Orta Oyunu* is an improvised farce resembling Italian commedia dell'arte and is full of mistaken identities and comic beatings using stock characters. *Orta Oyunu* means "played in the middle"; performers act in an open space surrounded by an audience.[18]

The Ottoman imperial period saw entertainments analogous to spectacles performed at European courts in the sixteenth and seventeenth centuries. The 1635 English translation of Baudier's *The History of the . . . Court of the Grand Seigneur Emparour of the Turkes* describes an Ottoman performance of a mock battle at the Hippodrome in Constantinople that ends when "they let slip into place about thirty Hogs which they had shut into a Fort and ranne after them crying and howling in mockerie: Thus the Turkes does not sport but in contemning the Christians, nor labour serious but in ruining them."[19] A victorious Ottoman Muslim identity was performed in contrast to a ridiculed Christian one. Such performances were the bread and circuses of the Ottoman Empire and were sometimes arranged to quiet a restive population: "Sometimes Turkish Sultans who had suffered defeat in battle, and with the idea of falsifying the reason for their defeat and retreat, and to erase from people's minds the sad impression left thereby, ordered great rejoicing and merriment on an unheard of scale . . . by celebrating splendid weddings of daughters or circumcision ceremonies of sons."[20]

Spectacles in the Hippodrome could serve an almost exclusively po-

Figure 3. From *The Song Contests of Turkish Minstrels: Improvised Poetry Sung to Traditional Music.* Copyright © Yildiray Erdener, *The Song Contests of Turkish Minstrels.*

litical purpose; Orta Oyunu, storytellers, and the like do not explicitly evoke Muslim worship, but neither do they invoke explicitly non-Islamic religious and ritual traditions. Turkish *ashiks*, however, perform almost completely outside of any Muslim religious context. Moreover, they retain elements of their pre-Islamic, shamanic past in Central Asia.

Before Turks started spending their free time watching movies and television, many passed long winter evenings in cafés entertained by musical performers known as ashiks. The ashik is a kind of minstrel with roots among the shamanic, Turkic peoples of Central Asia before they converted to Islam and moved westward. Indeed, the etymology of the English word "shaman" harks back to the Turkic *šaman*.[21] Ashiks play a long-necked, stringed instrument called a *saz* and sing and tell long tales of legendary heroes and lovers. The performance includes a mixture of memorized material and improvisation. Narratives of love and heroism are interspersed with proverbs, folk music, and political and social comments.[22] Sometimes, especially around Kars and Erzurum in northeastern Anatolia, more than one ashik performs and they engage in contests of improvised insults combined with tests of musical and vocal virtuosity.[23] They mix Islamic material with folk and legendary material (see figure 3).[24]

The ashik resembles a pagan shaman performing in the midst of Islami-cized populations in southwestern Asia. Natalie Moyle, in her book *The Turkish Minstrel Tale Tradition*, sees little difference between the ashik and the shaman: "The magical initiatory dreams of both professions [sha-man and minstrel] involve a profound experience of the sacred. Religious or ancestral figures appear to the dreamer and instill in him the gift of shamanizing or the gift of song."[25]

Moyle's book discusses the biography of a twentieth-century Turkish minstrel, Ashik Müdami. He had two dreams or trances that called him to become a minstrel. Moyle explains that this process is "strongly remi-niscent of Eliade's description of how a shaman accepts his calling. Min-strelsy resembles shamanism."[26] She goes on to say that

> Müdami claims to have seen the Prophet Mohammed and the fourth Ca-liph Ali in his dream and to have been given sherbet to drink. In Anatolian tradition, the magic elixir by which the religious figures confer the gift of song is also a love potion. The holy men of the dream show the future min-strel a girl who will be his beloved and his divinely sanctioned love for her and his art are inextricably intertwined. Surely it is no accident that *Aşık* in Turkish means not only "minstrel" but also "lover."[27] . . . Müdami repeat-edly points out how he is not himself, but the hero, when he is telling a minstrel tale. . . . One interesting aspect of both shamanizing and telling a minstrel tale is self-dramatization. The performer narrates and acts out that which he is experiencing.[28]

Similarly, in his book on Turkish minstrel song duels, Yildiray Erdener cites instances where Ashik Müdami and other famous minstrels were treated as shamans: they were asked to cure sick people, help find lost livestock, and promote bountiful crops and harvests.[29]

Ashik Müdami was very conscious of the tension between the pre-Islamic, shamanic nature of his calling as an ashik and the Muslim reli-gious milieu in which he lived and performed. His father was the village imam; Müdami kept his minstrelsy a secret from his father for two years before it was revealed by accident when his father attended an event where Müdami was performing. As Moyle writes, "His father . . . did not ap-prove of singing or playing musical instruments,"[30] and "even when he had become a recognized minstrel, Müdami would still introduce songs containing religious material by apologizing, 'My dear listeners, I know it is a sin to quote from the Koran with a saz in one's hand.'"[31]

The ashik tradition, though some of its material may be Islamicized, is a pre-Islamic artifact carried into the Muslim world from a shamanic past in Central Asia. Yildiray Erdener writes that ashiks combated clerical opposition to them by claiming that in their trance or dream, they were inspired by Muslim holy figures rather than pagan ones: "The bakshi of Central Asia, and especially his counterpart of Anatolia (the ashik) claimed that they received their poetic and musical inspiration directly from important Islamic figures such as the prophets, pirs, the Forty, or the Three Holy Ones, or from Hızır. Therefore, their profession, like the mullahs', was also linked to God."[32]

Turkic minstrelsy reconciled itself with Islam not by becoming a part of Muslim worship but by claiming that it had approval from the foundational figures of Islam. Müdami saw Muhammad and the caliph Ali in the dream that conferred the power of minstrelsy upon him. Before his dream Müdami says that he could not memorize the Koran, but afterward, though his reading skills were limited, he exhibited great verbal mastery in his oral performances.[33] Ta'ziyeh has been fully integrated into Iranian, Muslim worship, but the ashiks retain much of their pagan, pre-Islamic style and sanctify it by exchanging the pagan figure who inspires their music for a Muslim one. Indeed, ashiks normally wear suits and ties rather than the traditional Muslim dress of ta'ziyeh actors. In the Turkish social milieu they look more like secular Kemalists than practicing Muslims.[34]

Movies, television, and Western performance styles are putting indigenous Muslim performance in danger. Furthermore, the balance between piety and sacrilege is becoming less precarious in some parts of the Muslim world. Ta'ziyeh started out as a strictly religious ritual that became dramatic in the eighteenth century. Since the 1990s, the play has often been performed by Iranian companies outside of any Muslim religious context in major Western cultural centers: at the Avignon Festival in 1991, in Paris at the Festival d'Automne in 2000, at the Lincoln Center in New York in an air-conditioned circus tent in 2002 (complete with horses, camels, and sheep), and in Rome in 2003.[35] In these venues, ta'ziyeh has lost most of its religious and ritual character and become primarily a theatre piece. Audiences in New York and Paris applaud where audiences in early twentieth-century Iran wept and beat their chests.

Yildiray Erdener relates how one ashik, Ashik Reyhani, denied that his ability to sing and play and improvise came from a soul journey to the underworld. In an interview, Erdener asked him about the dream that inspired his minstrelsy and the ashik replied that the people of northeastern Turkey expect an ashik to have a dream. Ashik Reyhani told Erdener that the people believe in the dream and "they forced me to lie. . . . There is such a belief: if one sleeps at a grave yard or next to a creek Hızır [a traditional Muslim holy figure] would appear. People believed in this kind of story for centuries. . . . There are still people who believe in it. If I would deny it now they probably would throw stones at me."[36]

When Erdener spent a week with Ashik Reyhani at an international conference at the University of Michigan in Ann Arbor, Reyhani told him, "If there is someone who claims that he had a dream he is a liar, including me."[37] Reyhani is willing to suppose that ancient, legendary ashiks such as Yunus Emre or ashiks of the generation immediately preceding his own might have had the dream, though he expresses some doubt even about some of his older contemporaries, claiming that his and other ashiks' sacred, initiating dreams are phony—a matter of mere convention. Thus minstrelsy, like ta'ziyeh, appears to be moving away from its religious and ritual character to become aestheticized.

In spite of well-publicized, persistent, and virulent opposition to performance that currently persists among some Muslims (the Taliban of Afghanistan and Waziristan and the religious authorities in Saudi Arabia are well-known instances), the conflict between performance and Islam seems to be weakening. For ta'ziyeh and Turkish ashiks, the upshot is that the claims and compromises that defended ashik and ta'ziyeh performances against the charge of idolatry and sacrilege are falling by the wayside. Ta'ziyeh has become less a religious ritual and more a piece of theatre entertainment seen in international venues in countries such as France, Italy, and the United States. Still, theatrical and ritual performance continues sometimes to find itself in contested territory in the Muslim world. In contemporary Cairo, street theatre is performed on the occasion of the *Moulid* (also spelled *Mouled*) of Saida Aisha. A Moulid is the celebration of the birthday of a local saint or holy person. The neighborhood in Cairo known as Saida Aisha takes its name from a mosque named for a woman said to be a descendant of the Prophet Muhammad. She is supposed to have lived in the neighborhood and to have been buried there. Every year a festival celebrates her birthday. The festival includes a procession to the mosque with performances of farcical plays mounted on carts that pass through the busy streets. Normal traffic continues during the procession. One play represents a comic birth where the doctor delivers a puppy from a woman in labor. The play, after all, is performed in celebration of a birthday. In a television documentary on the Moulid,[38] residents of the neighborhood say that they perform because of their love for Saida Aisha and to honor the Prophet and his family. They say that they are doing theatre as an act of piety. They apparently want to justify what some might call an affront to their religion. In contemporary Cairo, just as in eighteenth-century Tehran or in an Anatolian coffeehouse, ritual and theatre are joined in a troubled place between piety and sacrilege.

Notes

1. The appropriate hadith, especially *Sahih Muslim* vol. 3, no. 5268, are discussed in many places. ReligionFacts at http://www.religionfacts.com/islam/things/depictions-of-muhammad-in-islamic-art.htm discusses the second commandment and Islam and cites the relevant hadith (2007).

2. Janet Afary, "Shi'ite Narratives of Karbala and Christian Rites of Penance: Michel Foucault and the Culture of the Iranian Revolution, 1978–9," in *Eternal Performance: Ta'ziyeh and Other Shiite Rituals*, ed. Peter J. Chelkowski (London: Seagull Books, 2010). Cited hereafter as "Chelkowski 2010." "Most scholars believe that the rituals have pre-Islamic origins. William Beeman argues that Muharram rituals are similar to those marking the death of Dionysus in Ancient Greek mythology, or Osiris in Ancient Egyptian mythology," Chelkowski 2010, 200. Metin And conjectures a possible link between the mourning cult for the imam Hussein and pre-Islamic cults of Attis, Adonis, and Osiris in *Drama at the Crossroads: Turkish Performing Arts Link Past and Present, East and West* (Istanbul: Isis Press, 1991), 22, 27–41.

3. Mayel Baktash discusses the imitation hadith in "Ta'ziyeh and Its Philosophy" in *Ta'ziyeh: Ritual and Drama in Iran*, ed. Peter J. Chelkowski (New York: New York University Press, 1979), 101–2. Cited hereafter as "Chelkowski 1979."

4. "In the past, actors read their lines from crib sheets held in their palms, indicating that they were merely role-carriers with no personal connections to the characters they portrayed. Today, most performers learn their roles by heart. . . . Influenced heavily by the realistic acting of modern film and television, Ta'ziyeh actors no longer distance themselves from the characters they are playing, but throw themselves wholeheartedly into their roles." Peter J. Chelkowski, "Time Out of Memory: Ta'ziyeh, the Total Drama," in Chelkowski 2010, 12. "The Ta'ziyeh art of acting makes the performer-believer a role carrier . . . , not a character." Andrzej Wirth, "Semiological Aspects of Ta'ziyeh," in Chelkowski 1979, 34.

5. And, *Drama at the Crossroads*, 115.

6. Iraj Anvar, "Peripheral Ta'ziyeh: The Transformation of Ta'ziyeh from Muharram Mourning Ritual to Secular and Comical Theatre," in Chelkowski 2010, 118.

7. "Spectators stand and join the performers in singing the refrain of the prayers that conclude some plays. When a protagonist announces that the time has arrived, or will soon arrive for . . . beating one's breast while singing appropriate verses of mourning—he may invite spectators to join in the ritual. As the protagonists weep and urge one another to weep or cease their weeping, many spectators are quite visibly and audibly weeping." Stephen Blum, "Compelling Reasons to Sing: The Music of Ta'ziyeh," in Chelkowski 2010, 171.

8. "A variety of Shiite sources, including the succeeding imams, emphasized that the weeping for Hussein and his family brings a reward in the hereafter and

that tears (and prayers) offered in this context will be rewarded at the Day of Judgement [*sic*]." Augustus Richard Norton, "Ritual, Blood, and Shiite Identity: Ashura in Nabatiyya, Lebanon," in Chelkowski 2010, 306. Norton cites Mahmoud Ayoub, *Redemptive Suffering in Islam: A Study of the Devotional Aspects of Ashura in Twelver Shiism* (The Hague: Mouton, 1978). Mayel Baktash also discusses weeping for Hussein as a sure way to paradise in "Ta'ziyeh and Its Philosophy" in Chelkowski 1979, 101–2.

9. Kamran Scot Aghaie, "The Origins of the Sunnite-Shiite Divide and the Emergence of the Ta'ziyeh Tradition," in Chelkowski 2010, 49. Aghaie is citing Jean Calmard quoting the relevant hadith: "Quiconque pleure pour Hussein ou fait pleurer pour Hussein entrera de droit au paradis," in "Le Patronage des Ta'ziyeh: Element pour une Étude Globale" in Chelkowski 1979, 122.

10. Peter J. Chelkowski, "Ta'ziyeh: Indigenous Avant-Garde Theatre of Iran," in Chelkowski 1979, 3–4; William O. Beeman and Mohammad B. Ghaffari, "Acting Styles and Actor Training in Ta'ziyeh," in Chelkowski 2010, 84.

11. See note 2 above.

12. Muhammad Ja'far Mahjub, "The Effect of European Theatre and the Influence of Its Theatrical Methods upon Ta'ziyeh," in Chelkowski 1979, 151.

13. Annemarie Schimmel, "The *Marsiyeh* in Sindhi Poetry," chap. 16 in Chelkowski 1979; Peter J. Chelkowski, "From the Sun-Scorched Desert of Iran to the Beaches of Trinidad: Ta'ziyeh's Journey from Asia to the Caribbean," in Chelkowski 2010, 408.

14. "Shiism is a religion of protest. It can only speak truth to power and destabilize it. It can never 'be in power.'" Hamid Dabashi, "Ta'ziyeh as Theatre of Protest," in Chelkowski 2010, 179. "Shiism is a religion of protest. It can never succeed politically without failing morally," 189.

15. "In the old city of Marrakesh, Ashura was observed as a happy day—puppets and acrobats in the main square, presents for children, sweets to everyone. 'This was the day that Sunnites triumphed,' explained a local merchant." Elizabeth Fernea, "Remembering the Ta'ziyeh in Iraq," in Chelkowski 2010, 296.

16. Baktash, "Ta'ziyeh and Its Philosophy," in Chelkowski 1979, 96–97.

17. Edmond Saussey, *Littérature Populaire Turque* (Paris: Études Orientales, 1936), 73–74; Metin And, *A History of Theatre and Popular Entertainment in Turkey* (Ankara: Forum Yayinlari, 1963–64), 28–31.

18. Saussey, *Littérature Populaire*, 74–82; And, *History of Theatre*, 25–28.

19. Cited by And, *History of Theatre*, 19–20.

20. And, *History of Theatre*, 17.

21. Berthold Laufer, "Origin of the Word Shaman," *American Anthropologist*, New Series 19, no. 3 (July–September 1917): 361–71.

22. Metin And, *Culture, Performance and Communication in Turkey* (Tokyo: Institute for the Study of Languages and Cultures of Asia and Africa, 1987), 74–78. İlhan Başgöz discusses variety in *ashik* performances in "Digression in Oral Narrative" in *Turkish Folklore and Oral Literature: Selected Essays of İlhan Başgöz*, ed. Kemal Silay (Bloomington, IN: Indiana University Turkish Studies, 1998), 231ff.

23. Yildiray Erdener, in *The Song Contests of Turkish Minstrels: Improvised Poetry Sung to Traditional Music* (New York: Garland, 1995), especially emphasizes *ashik* competition.

24. "The *aşık* gives the same importance to folk poetry and legend as he gives to quotations from the holy Koran and to prayers." And, *Culture, Performance and Communication*, 76.

25. Natalie Kononenko Moyle, *The Turkish Minstrel Tale Tradition* (New York: Garland, 1990), 64.

26. Ibid., 59. Yildiray Erdener also makes this point in *Song Contests*, 49. Like Moyle, he also cites Mircea Eliade's *Shamanism*, trans. Willard R. Trask (Princeton, NJ: Princeton University Press), 67.

27. Moyle, *Turkish Minstrel*, 65.

28. Ibid., 67.

29. Erdener, *Song Contests*, 68.

30. Moyle, *Turkish Minstrel*, 56.

31. Ibid., 57.

32. Erdener, *Song Contests*, 52–53.

33. Moyle, *Turkish Minstrel*, 57–58.

34. In 1925 Ataturk gave a famous speech in which he demonstrated the wearing of the fedora and passed a "hat law" that made the wearing of the fez a criminal offense. He also banned the veil and generally promoted European dress in the new Turkish Republic. Bernard Lewis, *The Emergence of Modern Turkey* (London: Oxford University Press, 1968), 268–71. In contemporary Turkey, secular Kemalists have been scandalized by the fact that the wives of both the prime minister and the president wear headscarves. Until recently headscarves and beards were banned in state buildings. The army is a traditional supporter of modernity and secularism. A wedding invitation that I received in 1999 from a former Turkish student stipulated that since the ceremony was to take place on an army base, women wearing headscarves and men wearing beards would not be admitted. The invitation was in English and Turkish. The English version did not include this stipulation.

35. Chelkowski 2010 contains several chapters devoted to these performances.

36. Erdener, *Song Contests*, 58–59.

37. Ibid.

38. El-Warsha produced the documentary in 1994. *El-Warsha* means "the workshop" and is the name of an experimental theatre group in Cairo. All the information about the Moulid of Saida Aisha in this discussion is from the documentary.

Cave Rituals and the Brain's Theatre

Mark Pizzato

THE TERM "theatre" comes from the ancient Greek *theatron*, the "seeing place" for the audience. But theatre in its most basic sense, as the space and activity of a spectator and a performer with reflective awareness between them, extends much further back into prehistory. Such reflective awareness of Self and Other in performance also relates to the theatres of imagination, memories, dreams, and reality representations within the brains of each actor and spectator. This inner theatre extends back to prehistory, too, with brain structures that we have inherited along with evolving rituals of transcendence and reflective performance spaces.

A primal form of theatrical performance and awareness of Self and Other emerged in certain caves thirty-two thousand to eleven thousand years ago during the Ice Age (or Upper Paleolithic Period), as evidenced by the art on the cave walls and other artifacts. One of the earliest, with some of the finest art, is shown in Werner Herzog's 2010 3-D documentary film *Cave of Forgotten Dreams*. It explores prehistoric art in the Chauvet Cave in France, which was discovered in 1994 and has since been off-limits to the public. This essay considers that film and cave, plus details from lesser-known caves in France and Spain, which I visited in June 2011.[1] Such caves offer evidence of a primal form of reflective performance: the evolution of human subjectivity based in, yet moving beyond, primate playfulness through shared emotions, neural filters, and simulations of the Other. How did the selection of specific cave spaces for paintings and engravings on the walls, along with the types of images made, express not only the performances in them but also the birth of a distinct sense of Self, of human character being like and unlike observed animals, using the cave wall as a map and mirror?

Theories of Cave Theatre

In his recent book, *Palaeoperformance*, and in earlier essays, Yann-Pierre Montelle explores the evidence for many aspects of theatricality in the prehistoric caves of France: not only the paintings, etchings, and carvings on the rock walls but also the various sizes and shapes of caverns; the bone flutes, scrapers, and bullroarers found in them; and the resonant tones produced today by tapping stalactites of different lengths.[2] Prior to Montelle, Jean Clottes and David Lewis-Williams developed a theory, based on such evidence along with neuroscience research and anthropological comparisons with recent African traditions, that prehistoric cave art shows the recording, display, and ritual use of hallucinatory trance experiences involving animal-spirit guides.[3] Ice Age peoples may have produced cave art through visions that occurred spontaneously in the extreme darkness with its echoing sounds, evoked by the flickering fires of torches and animal-fat lamps, painful treks deep into the earth, loss of oxygen and increase of other gases, and the rock's natural shapes and crevices.[4] Shamanic drugs might also have been involved. The mysterious geometric lines and dots in prehistoric cave art, along with realistic animal figures and hybrid human-animal creatures, correspond to the types and stages of hallucinatory visions that can be evoked today in the laboratory through sensory deprivation or flashing lights. Such hallucinations, though now involving objects in our own cultural context, are also experienced by people with migraines and other disorders. Thus, cave art may reveal two possible manifestations of prehistoric theatre: (1) visionary experiences of geometric, abstract, and supernatural figures from within a human brain projected onto or through the rock surface and (2) shared performances in the cave using the rock art as scenic background, mythic illustrations, or moving characters in the firelight and its shadows.

The types of cave-art spaces also demonstrate various aspects of prehistoric theatre. Some are easily accessible in huge chambers. Others are hundreds of meters inside the earth, requiring crouched walking or crawling through narrow passages. In more accessible chambers, processions and large ritual gatherings may have occurred. But for those with tight corridors deep into the darkness, with slippery surfaces, low ceilings, and sudden cliffs, and with bears, hyenas, and lions potentially present, great courage and painful ordeals were involved for a few individuals—perhaps shamanic leaders putting initiates through transformative nightmares. Montelle relates this to male initiation rites practiced historically by various tribes elsewhere in the world.[5] Combining Montelle's argument on initiation rites, Clottes and Lewis-Williams's theory of individual and collective visions of rock art as a supernatural membrane, and my own experiences underground and with Herzog's film, I will give details from specific caves, showing the possible origins of human theatricality in distinctive forms of awareness of Self and Other.

A Cave Onscreen

In Herzog's film, his voice-over calls Chauvet "proto-cinema," for this cave shows some of the earliest and finest paintings yet discovered. Some are carbon-dated at thirty-two thousand years old. Various animal figures have three-dimensional shading in the legs, bellies, and heads. There are many overlapping and echoing images, suggesting movement and perhaps scenes of predation (with lions stalking bison and rhinos) or of sparring (with rhinos knocking horns).[6] Yet most of Chauvet's figures, as in the caves of France and Spain that I visited, are floating on the rock surfaces, not tied to contextual scenes or obvious narratives. This indicates very personal, dreamlike visions in the paintings rather than general representations of reality outside the cave. But they may also contain a collective language of symbols and imagery that we can no longer read.

The etchings are stunning, too; detailed images of horses and other large animals are cut into the rock as white outlines against the darker surface layer and use the natural curves of the walls, like the paintings. (The 3-D technology in Herzog's film enhances the viewer's experience of this.) Such etchings, in Chauvet and the caves that I personally visited, suggest a more immediate artistic impulse, perhaps outlining on the wall the animals and other supernatural figures seen in or through the rock during shamanic trances. Later, some of the etchings were painted with black or red outlines, and sometimes with more detailed shadings and interactions using black charcoal or manganese rock and red or yellow ocher. "Crayon" sticks of such materials and colors have been found in some caves. Mineral pigments were also ground into powder, mixed with liquid, and painted with a brush or sprayed from the mouth, sometimes using the bone tubes that have been found. This technology, along with the scaffolding needed for paintings five meters high in caves such as Font-de-Gaume (fifteen thousand years ago), required prior planning and materials collected in or brought into the cave. The carved sculptural reliefs in rock shelters like Abri du Cap Blanc (of horses, fifteen thousand years ago) would have taken even more time to produce. Yet the numerous overlapping engravings in many caves might have been created quickly, in direct response to personal visions, and then shared with others in that form or with further artistic elaborations, showing a spectrum from individual to collective theatre experiences.[7]

Herzog's film involves interviews with scientists working at Chauvet, including a statement by Jean Clottes that Upper Paleolithic peoples were different from us in their perception of reality as supernatural, with "fluidity" between human, animal, and nonanimal forms and with "permeability" between performance spaces, rock walls, and other worlds. And yet this fluid and permeable context for prehistoric art, akin to how we may experience the Chauvet Cave through cinema, or other caves in person, suggests a continuity between us and humans (whose brains were anatomically "modern" like ours) tens of thousands of years ago. We enter the cinema chamber in near darkness and become transported through the images on the wall. We add personal associations, memories, and fantasies to the figures onscreen, while photos on a filmstrip, repeated yet subtly changing at twenty-four frames per second, evoke the illusion of movement in our heads. With or without 3-D technology and glasses, we see a much more fluid and permeable world in the movie theatre than is really there in the images onscreen, the acoustics around us, and the lures of cinematic cuts, moving camera shots, and diegetic framings.

Seeing a photograph of cave art, or a film documentary of Chauvet, does not convey the experience of being inside a cave with prehistoric theatrical imagery. Still, Herzog's film illustrates how humans have experienced theatre for at least thirty-two thousand years, extending the inner performance spaces of reality perceptions, memories, fantasies, and dreams toward shared artistic, ritual, and entertainment events. In particular, the multiple echoing images of horse heads, or of a single repeated head, of rhino heads with horns and partial body outlines, and of lion heads on the walls of Chauvet show a prehistoric, theatrical, and cinematic impulse to present various moments together at once, collapsing and yet extending time and space.

There are also distinctive chambers in Chauvet, as shown in the Herzog film, that suggest ritualized spaces. On a large rounded stalactite, hanging from the center of the rock ceiling in the deepest cavern with paintings, are the black outlines of a woman's legs (no feet) and vulva, akin to those on carved figurines that have been found in Germany, such as the "Venus of Willendorf." Yet there is also a dark, filled-in bison head just above the vulva and legs, as if emerging from them, or as if a bison-man with one leg (and perhaps a human hand) was overlapping the woman's. A lion's head and body emerges from the other side of the woman's legs. Around this central stalactite painting are many images on the walls, including vulvas and the repeated animal-head images described above. All this indicates that Chauvet was not just a prehistoric art gallery but also a theatre for gendered, supernatural myths and rites.

Another chamber, which "resembles an amphitheatre," contains further evidence for ritual performances in Chauvet.[8] A bear skull placed on a flat rock has charcoal markings dated to thirty thousand years ago, and there are dozens of other bear skulls around it, including one with black lines. These suggest a staging of the meanings of life and death, human and animal, and predator and prey related to the many paintings and engravings throughout the cave: lions, bears, rhinos, horses, bison, ibexes, reindeer, and mammoths (including one with a thin chest and strangely rounded feet). This artwork may have been inspired by the spectacular natural formations of the cave—its huge columns, cake-like stalagmite mounds, needle-pointed stalactites, and rock curtains glistening with calcite crystals. The cave today, like others with prehistoric art in southern France and northern Spain, conveys the sense of a majestic cathedral, with high arches and spires drawing the eye upward, womblike openings, and painted figures that may reflect ancestral totem spirits that possessed performers who embodied them for others, or entered the minds of visual artists who left such images for us as the Other.

Caves in Spain

In the Tito Bustillo Cave, across the Pyrenees and far to the west of Chauvet, in the Asturias region of northern Spain, the artwork was created over a long stretch of time, from twenty thousand to twelve thousand years ago, with most of it made fifteen thousand to fourteen thousand years ago. One chamber with a very narrow opening has on its walls red triangular signs that perhaps have mythic, performative meanings, like the Chauvet stalactite. This room has been dubbed the "Chamber of Vulvas," although the mysterious signs look more like hoofprints to me. Maybe they reflect a hunter's imagination, tracking the deer, bison, and horses that are represented in outline or with fully shaded forms elsewhere in the cave. The evidence from bones left at Cro-Magnon (Paleolithic human) campsites shows that the killing and eating of such large animals was a rarity during the Ice Age.[9] Yet the theory of Henri Breuil from half a century ago, that the cave art demonstrated an attempt to wield the power of hunting magic over such animals, might still bear some validity, especially if these were rare and prized game. Indeed, there are black outlines of bison and horses on a red background in Tito Bustillo, which is unusual for Paleolithic cave art.[10] The red wash, painted first, might represent blood or the living tissue of the animal's inner body, as experienced by hunters. Within the legs of some of the figures, the red paint also suggests an exploration of musculature, using the natural texture of the rock. Perhaps this involved shamanic performances of animal spirits as well, with an animated human actor wearing an animal skin and mask, as in many tribal cultures around the world.

The famous cave of Altamira, near Santillana del Mar, about a ninety-minute drive east of Tito Bustillo, also has red and black shading within its black outlines of bison, but only a little red wash behind them in some areas. At least that is my perception from photos and a life-size reproduction of Altamira's main polychrome chamber, since the actual cave is now closed to the public due to damage to the art from bacteria brought in by twentieth-century visitors (as with France's Lascaux).[11] The paintings also use natural round protrusions in the cave's ceiling to depict very detailed, curled bison that look as if they were sleeping there. Perhaps both active and sleeping (or dying) animals were envisioned through the rock membrane and performed in this cave.[12] Campsite evidence near the entrance of Altamira shows Ice Age peoples living there twenty-two thousand to thirteen thousand years ago; the art is dated at sixteen thousand to fourteen thousand years ago.

At the smaller El Buxu Cave (to the west, nearer to Tito Bustillo), there is also evidence close to the cave's entrance of prehistoric habitation twenty thousand to eighteen thousand years ago. Deeper inside the cave, through a one-meter crawl space (with a lower floor now for modern visitors), there is a chamber with etched and black-outlined goats on a natural arch. Farther inside, mat-like forms have been etched over the outlines of deer, as if covering them or performing magic upon them. In that area there is also a red, sideways *E*. Even farther into the cave, the most detailed horses are drawn, plus more goats and a large fallow deer above them. These etchings are very difficult to make out until the Spanish guide, like a modern shaman, outlines them with the shadow of a finger or a red laser pointer, etching the images into the viewer's brain as well.[13]

Somewhat near El Buxu and Tito Bustillo, the El Pindal Cave entrance has a wonderful view of the Atlantic from a cliff overlooking the sea, though in prehistoric times the water level was much lower, so the view would have been different. Along the walls inside the cave, which has no evidence of habitation, there are significant red animal outlines and markings. Moving into the depths one finds: a *P* and some triangles (perhaps akin to the vulva or hoof marks in Tito Bustillo); bison and a horse that involve the natural concave surfaces; abstract outlines and repeated "claviforms" (key or club shapes like the *P*); many dots; a deer or goat figure with hash marks on the rock ledge over it; and five vertical lines crossed by two thick horizontal ones. There is also the outline of a mammoth with a red spot outside it and another mammoth nearby with a similar spot inside it (both facing deeper into the cave), which may depict a vision of soul or heart inside and outside of the huge beast, or a hunter's target for killing it. But the relationship seems to transcend hunting, since such an encounter would have been a very rare event. Only three mammoth depictions have been found in the caves of northern Spain (but there are more in France, especially in the black outlines of Rouffignac). The artwork here is from twenty thousand to fourteen thousand years ago.

These caves, along with others I describe below, show a long-term engagement with animal figures, floating on cave-wall surfaces as paintings or etchings. Ice Age humans must have identified more with animals in their environment than we do today, since they were struggling to survive, like them, as predators and prey, in very harsh conditions. Performances with cave art—as isolated experiences of visions in narrow caverns such as El Buxu, or with more collective rituals in larger cave spaces such as Tito Bustillo, Altamira, and El Pendal—probably involved both shadow play, as in Plato's parable of the cave, and redefinitions of character, as in Lacan's mirror stage.[14] But if they were seeking ideal truths beyond the cave's hallucinatory shadows and artistic images, prehistoric peoples were going deep inside, through the rock wall and its crevices, rather than outside to the sunlight, as in Plato's myth. They may have been exploring something ontologically prior to Plato's antitheatrical prejudice and his suspicions about art luring us away from truth. While inventing visual art on the cave walls, they were also exploring transformations of identity: from mimetic emotions and movements shared with animals from the environment outside the cave, to finding a theatrical sense of Self through Other spirits, recorded and displayed on the rock surfaces.

Portable works of art have also been found in many caves, such as El Pendo in Cantabria, which has evidence of Neanderthal and then human habitation, from eighty-four thousand years ago until the Bronze Age. Occasional floods of rainwater into the cave's large mouth, and many fallen rocks, make excavations of the different layers of occupation difficult. But in the Paleolithic layer hundreds of deer horns with various engravings have been found, including a rare snake representation, as well as jaws eating a deer etched into bone from twenty thousand years ago and a thin human female etched onto another bone (unlike the fat "Venus" sculptures found elsewhere). A Cro-Magnon child's skull was also found. There are dozens of paintings from the same time period deeper inside the cave, beyond the reach of sunlight, along one twenty-five-meter wall and another nine-meter wall. The higher paintings would have required wooden scaffolding, as at Font-de-Gaume. But the red paintings later became covered with black bacteria, making them difficult to see even after the walls were cleaned in modern times. There is a red deer with a small head, filled in with fingertip dots of paint and yet empty at the center, perhaps suggesting pregnancy. There is also an incomplete horse without a head, a bull, and the disembodied head of a deer, plus two deer facing outward in opposite directions, one with a long neck, the other with front legs up as if leaping. Another painting of a deer uses a crack in the rock for its back. There is a possible snake form, too, and one deer head inside the outline of another deer, at its front quarters. Thus, in this cave one can see partial remnants of a large gallery of prehistoric works of art, on the walls and in mobile objects left in the cave. They reflect the inner theatres of many human brains, mirroring various forms of the animal Other, like figures from dreams.

More elaborate red paintings, and perhaps an anamorphic image, appear in the narrower passages of the Covalanas Cave, which is also in Cantabria.[15] Its rock formations include fossils of marine animals such as seahorses, strange calcite cubes, and swirled surfaces produced over the millennia by ocean and rain water rushing or seeping through the earth. But it has no evidence of habitation. Its artwork dates from twenty thousand years ago and is more vividly experienced, as with the Niaux Cave in France, because the cave is unlit except by visitors' flashlights. (Radioactive uranium in the calcite that formed naturally under and over some of the Covalanas artwork allows for objective, not just stylistic, dating.) A panel of rock shows a group of six female deer outlined in red, though they appear only gradually, through the guide's tracings: a deer with a long neck, painted around a protruding rock for her stomach (perhaps suggesting pregnancy); a deer outlined with fingertip dots like in El Pendo; the full outline of a deer with legs in perspective; another deer with head turned and body colored in; and two deer with necks overlapping that face opposite directions, so that one is clearly behind the other.

This mix of figures in faint red outlines and dim light appears fragmentary, like etchings in other caves (especially the many overlapping lines in France's Combarelles Cave). The fragments that form wholes but are again cut up by overlapping outlines may reflect the illusory formation of the Self (the imago of an ideal ego) in the Lacanian mirror stage, masking the contrary experience of an alienated, uncoordinated, libidinous "body in pieces." This occurs in infancy, as shown by the jubilation of the child in the mirror, but it also repeats throughout one's life, with numerous desires of the Other, on stages, mirrors, and screens that offer the vision of a whole Self. Thus, one can see mirror-stage reflections of the prehistoric mind as an internal theatre, or "intra-organic mirror,"[16] in caves such as Covalanas, with the emergence of a new form of human identity tens of thousands of years ago, similar to yet beyond the perspectives of other animals.[17]

On the opposite wall from that six-deer panel is an aurochs (Ice Age bull) with the edge of the rock as its back. There are other deer farther into the cave, and then a horse with detailed mandible and mane. To the left and below it are a red colored-in triangle (or female sign) and three deer. On the opposite wall, under a rock curtain, is another deer with long neck and legs lifted as if leaping. There are big deer on the inside of that curtain, plus a filled-in triangle on top of a box (perhaps a phallic sign). And then, in a narrow passage wide enough for just three people, another deer appears. But its full form with a white calcite eye is seen only at a distant angle from down the passageway, like the anamorphic illusions in later Western paintings, such as the two-dimensional skull in Hans Holbein's *The Ambassadors*, which becomes three-dimensional when viewed at an angle. Lacan uses this skull as an example of how "consciousness, in its illusion of *seeing itself seeing itself*, finds its basis in the inside-out structure of the gaze," an object reflecting the mortal lack of being in the subject.[18] One could also see this illusory nature of human consciousness in Covalanas, emerging distinctively twenty thousand years ago with the gaze of the shamanic artist or spectator reflected in the eye of the deer as Other. Perhaps it is a "phallic ghost," as Lacan says about the Holbein skull, signifying the lack of being (and the desire to be) in mankind's evolution beyond a natural environment, transforming it through art and culture.

Another Cantabrian cave, El Castillo, shows evidence of being inhabited as much as 120,000 years ago by Neanderthals and then, more recently, by prehistoric humans. The original entrance was a tight crawl space, but it is now deeply excavated into a wide opening, and there is an interpretive center nearby. Deeper inside, a large chamber has horses outlined in red on a flat, cracked surface as well as partial outlines of deer and bison floating on the rock canvas and pointing downward. There is also a thirty-thousand-year-old black bison pointing down, with a small deer coming out of its back and a red negative handprint on its left. (The term "negative handprint" refers to the Paleolithic practice of putting a hand against the rock and blowing or brushing paint around it, leaving its imprint as negative space within the painting. A "positive handprint" involves putting paint on the hand and then placing it on the rock.) Lower down, in a wide chamber, a bison is outlined in red, with negative handprints below it on its left. More art can be found farther inside, including the print of a right hand made with the back of the hand to the wall; two bison in black outline on a ledge of rock; a smaller chamber with the outline of an aurochs; horizontal spots; another aurochs; spots in the shape of a horn; and then, after ten meters of blank wall, some diamond shapes with kite-like tails. There are additional images deeper inside the cave that are not accessible to the public. The large chambers in El Castillo would allow many people to participate in ritual performances, though there is a steep grade within and between some of the areas. The sixty handprints throughout the cave may be some kind of formal sign system, or perhaps they just signify playfulness or proclaim "I was here" (probably all of these and more).

Language, identity, and play are key elements in the new form of human mind that evolved with cave art.[19] According to cognitive psychologist Merlin Donald, our hominid ancestors went through several stages of cognitive and cultural evolution: from episodic animal consciousness toward mimetic communication with kinetic gestures and playfulness in *Homo erectus* two million years ago; to a mythic culture with verbal language in *Homo sapiens* half a million years ago; to a theoretical culture of technology and art forty thousand years ago, as evidenced by the caves and mobile artwork.[20] We still pass through these levels of consciousness, communication, and identity today as we grow from childhood to adulthood, and they form layers of our internal and external theatres. Archaeologist Stephen Mithen gives a similar timeline and adds that humans about forty thousand years ago evolved a new "cognitive fluidity" between various types of intelligence that had been isolated in the hominid brain before that: natural history intelligence (such as interpreting animal hoofprints), social intelligence (communicating intentionally), and technical intelligence (producing artifacts from mental templates).[21] This led to new productions of symbolic meanings and artwork that combined natural, social, and technical mappings—and performances—of inner and outer worlds involving animal, human, and abstract figures.

It also involved music. The Las Monedas Cave, a short walk from El Castillo, has many geological spectacles and a small area of humanmade art, with a smiling reindeer, horses, a fox, a bison, and various other shapes from twelve thousand years ago. On my tour of the cave, the guide illustrated its performative qualities by tapping several hollow stalactites of varying sizes with his knuckle like a xylophone (or "lithophone," as he called it), showing the different notes they contained and the soft echoes of the cavern, as if in a small concert hall. He also pointed out the much larger organ-like columns closer to the entrance of the cave, suggesting the musical possibilities in larger caverns as well.

Hornos de la Peña, which is also in Cantabria, offers a very different experience. One has to crouch or crawl with the guide into very small chambers (some with room for just a few people), where there are mostly etchings, but also a few paintings. A horse and aurochs are engraved in an area near the entrance, which was inhabited twenty-eight thousand years ago. Then there is a tight space to crawl through into a somewhat larger chamber, which might hold a dozen people, where another horse is engraved on the wall, along with "macaroni" finger fluting (produced by human fingers moving through the soft clay of the cave in straight or wavy lines), a goat from twenty thousand to eighteen thousand years ago (its eye using the rock's natural indentation), and a bison from fifteen thousand years ago. Deeper inside the cave, on one side of a small chamber, are a goat and more abstract lines from thirty to twenty-eight thousand years ago, with larger horses and a deer head to the right, plus a possible serpent figure. Above the horses is an anthromorph: a human figure with a bird's head, a raised hand, and a tail, from twenty thousand years ago. Nearby is a horse covered with crosshatches, and another horse on the low ceiling has a hole in its stomach or womb. The guide explained that *horno* means "oven" and is also a reference to "womb" in Spanish, as in the English phrase "she has one in the oven."

Entering this cave, with its small chambers and intriguing engravings, and crawling (sometimes backward) out make the experience womb-like. In Plato's and Kristeva's (Lacanian) sense the space becomes a *chora*: an enclosed space of becoming for the subject aesthetic and imaginary via the art on the walls as performative, interpretive mirrors. The Self of each visitor today is changed to some degree by performing with the guide and others in the small group who squeeze their bodies into that space within the earth and perceive the paintings and etchings as lines and scratches in the rock made tens of thousands of years ago, which gain gestalt forms once again. Although we live in a very different world now, with mass-media screens, electric lights, climate-controlled homes, food in grocery stores, vehicles for speedy travel, and many other transformations of the environment, we can find a kinship with prehistoric ancestors (or their European relatives) through such cave theatres. We can glimpse how their sense of Self was emerging through reflections on animal and human nature in the various reptilian and mammalian forms and the peculiar bird-man with a tail in this cave as a chora, "where the subject is both generated and negated."[22] Or, in Mithen's terms, we can see the prehistoric mind, with its cognitive fluidity, creating imaginative and sometimes hybrid creatures as characters for Self and Other, yet also seeking a "cognitive anchor" in the cave images or symbols, as in later religious art and ritual performances involving various iconic images.[23]

Caves in France

There are various caves in France (like Chauvet) with elaborate artistic expressions that I have written about elsewhere: Lascaux, Font-de-Gaume, Combarelles, Rouffignac, Cougnac, Pech Merle, and Niaux. But there are also smaller French caves, which I visited in 2011, with details worth considering.

The Merveilles Cave is located near a popular tourist site, the medieval cliffside town of Rocamadour (well worth a visit as well). The cave was inhabited twenty thousand years ago and has some interesting natural formations, along with paintings and etchings near the entrance, mostly in a single large chamber. But they are difficult to see, even with the guide's help. There is a negative handprint over a deer that appears to be leaping through a white calcite barrier, although that may have formed in the thousands of years after the artwork was made. (The natural spectacles in various caves considered here—stalactites, stalagmites, columns, and drapes—grew very gradually, taking thousands of years to form.) To the right of that handprint and deer is a stag with an oversized head, a horse facing the opposite direction, a strange negative handprint with six fingers, a big horse, and perhaps a hyena.

Gargas, a cave in the Pyrenees,[24] has handprints as well as animal outlines and etchings from the beginning of the cave-art era, thirty thousand years ago. There is a child's negative handprint near the small living area by the original entrance, and many adult hands deeper inside the cave, especially on one wall. Another handprint appears at the opening to an inner chamber (which is off-limits to visitors today) and has a red spot on the other side, perhaps signifying something about that inner space. There are a total of 231 handprints in the cave, with 124 clearly visible and just 10 of those having all their fingers.[25] Over half of the hands are missing all four fingers and have just a thumb showing. None have a missing thumb. This may signify the importance of an opposable thumb, or it may be some other hand sign language that we cannot read today. But the art throughout the cave also seems to start with a child's gesture near a campsite home at the cave's entrance, perhaps just making a playful handprint before it became an adult performance rite, which might have involved, as Lewis-Williams theorizes, the hands disappearing into the rock wall and communing with the spirits there as they were painted over, leaving the negative print.[26]

Primatologists have observed that humans exhibit neoteny: we look and behave like young apes.[27] Adult humans, with round heads and flat faces, extend youthful play into many performance activities, from theatre to sports to video games, while also displaying the curiosity and inventiveness that led to vast transformations of culture and environment in prior generations. Prehistoric artists may have had very serious reasons for painting their hands onto the cave wall, especially with missing fingers. Some paleontologists today speculate that the fingers were lost due to frostbite or disease or were deliberately cut off in sacrificial rites. But it is more likely that the cave artists were displaying the significance of digits, as present or absent, by bending their fingers while making the handprints to make the prints appear fingerless. Such playfulness in the art, behind whatever symbolic language the prints might have had, shows a crucial element in the growing flexibility of our human ancestors as big-brained apes. For better and worse, humans found ways to survive and reproduce far beyond natural instincts by playing with their inner drives and brain theatres,[28] projecting them outward as spirits and cave images and eventually changing the world. But then the problem became, as it still is now, how to limit human creativity and destructiveness in the further performance spaces—of a ritual and technological chora—beyond the cave.

North of the main cave-art area around Lascaux, the Villars Cave has spectacular natural features, including needlelike stalactites and rock drapery, that are enhanced by the tour's sound-and-light show.[29] The guide takes visitors through a low, narrow passage to a half-dozen black horse outlines, including one that has changed to blue over the millennia and has a few millimeters of natural white calcite covering it. Close to the cave's prehistoric entrance, a wall painting shows a bison apparently charging at a thinly drawn man, almost a stick figure, whose hand extends over his head, perhaps in fear or to provoke the bison or to exert magic power over it.[30]

The art here is recent compared to Chauvet and Gargas; it is from about eighteen to seventeen thousand years ago, almost as close to our time as it is to the artwork of those other caves. This approaches the end of the Paleolithic cave-art period in Europe and the start of the Neolithic agricultural revolution, which began eleven thousand years ago in Mesopotamia and led to the domestication of certain prey animals whose images are in the caves: goats, aurochs, and horses. They were captured in ways other than artistic representation and turned to other uses as humans created increasingly large settlements, and then civilizations, which involved the storage of wealth and a warrior class and weaponry to defend it or take it away from others. As the Judeo-Christian scriptures put it later, mankind gained "dominion" over the animals, through God's creative will. Yet some animals, such as charging bison, could still be a threat. The cognitive anchors of religious beliefs, with gods as super-parental figures (perhaps deriving from cave images), imposed limits on the reckless playfulness of the human ape and conceptual constraints to its big-brained plasticity. Such beliefs, making up for the lack of instinctual patterns of perception and behavior in our species, are still needed by many today, even as science has provided other cognitive anchors in the last half millennium—though both have also led to great destructiveness, as well as creativity and good works, in the theatres beyond the cave.

Pair-non-Pair, north of Bordeaux, had a small prehistoric entry hole that required crawling but prevented bears from entering the cave. Inside, a humanmade ring protrudes from the low stone ceiling, perhaps for an animal-skin curtain as a barrier against the cold. Such evidence of habitation at the entrance of this cave and others relates to the steady temperature farther inside, near sixty degrees Fahrenheit all year, as compared to the Ice Age extremes outside. A second chamber beyond the entryway contains etchings (plus a hole above, giving light), and a third has a natural spring and pool, a vent in the rock ceiling for a campfire, and more engravings. With the help of the guide, one can find a mammoth with a goat above it, a bison, and several horses. Two of the horses have long necks and one has an open mouth, looking back toward the pool. One also finds a *Megaloceros* (giant elk) and a large horse over it that make use of differences in the natural rock colors for shading. Seashells in the rock are used for the eyes of the horse and mammoth. This cave was inhabited over a long period, from eighty to eighteen thousand years ago, by Neanderthals and humans. The art is from thirty thousand years ago, in the earliest period of cave theatres, like Chauvet.

Ice Age humans probably saw their own faces less than we do today. But with a pool of water inside this cave, infants could experience the mirror stage in its horizontal surface, as well as through their mother's touch, smell, cooing, and facial expressions. The further imaging of Self and Other through perceptions and etchings of animal figures on the cave walls may relate to the good fortune people felt in finding this cave, where they could live with a campfire, water, shelter, and a steady temperature. The engraving of the horse with a long neck and open mouth, looking back at the pool, may speak to this, and to touch, sound, movement, and vision as aspects of performance in the small ritual spaces of this cave theatre.

A Final Question and Some Conclusions

Why are there very few human images in prehistoric cave paintings (other than handprints)—and none in the finely detailed, lifelike style of certain animals in Chauvet, Lascaux, Font-de-Gaume, Niaux, and Altamira?[31] Findings from neuroscience about aspects of the brain's anatomy and its basic functions that we share with humans tens of thousands of years ago, along with the evidence of various theatrical spaces and images in the caves, may provide an answer.

Neurologist Antonio Damasio has developed a model of human Self-consciousness emerging from brain and mind, in contrast with other animals.[32] He defines a "protoself," which is found primarily in the brain stem, nervous system, and sensory portals, involves interior functions and body mapping, and offers visceral feelings of self; a "core self," found in the subject and object mappings and dispositions of cortical sensory and association areas, with convergent-divergent regions for monitoring body-to-world relations; and an "autobiographical self," which is centered in the posterior medial cortex and prefrontal lobes and involves image salience, memory edits, and future plans, along with conscious Self-reflection and a "Theory of Mind" about others. "Theory of Mind" is the phrase used by primatologists and neuroscientists for the human ability, starting at the age of four and going far beyond the ability of other apes, to form theories about other persons' perspectives.[33] This involves a "mirror neuron system" in the human brain, with certain cells firing both when an action is performed and when it is observed being done by another person (or animal), in ways beyond other primates (though it was initially discovered in monkeys).[34] Mirror neurons, along with canonical neurons (firing with typical objects for certain actions) and intuition neurons (firing when emotions are shared), form "simulations" within one's brain of what might be going on inside another person's brain in each social situation.[35]

Thus, the performances of everyday life involve "emotional contagion" between brains, often at a subconscious level, as in a wild herd, pack, or flock, moving collectively, with individuals reacting to subtle cues from others.[36] Simulations in the human brain's inner theatre mirror another's actions, facial expressions, gestures, vocal tones, and phonemes, beyond (or beneath) verbal language. Our brain theatres play the character of the other we observe or interact with, sending signals to perform the other's actions and emotions as "somatic markers" (in Damasio's phrase) of the other's thoughts and feelings—as if I am the other, in order to understand the other's perspective as like and unlike my own. Usually, I have a sense of my own character that filters and inhibits such mimicry at the overt level, unless I want to mimic the other. This is especially so in the dominant convention for Euro-American spectators: I watch the show while staying in my seat, participating vicariously. Even with my brain sending signals to mimic the movements and emotions onstage, I remain still (like most people while dreaming, when motor and emotion circuits are active but the body's movements are inhibited). Yet some people suffer from "echopraxia" due to damage in the "braking mechanism" of the frontal lobes and compulsively mimic others.[37]

So, the human sense of Self in our ancestors emerged from a proto-to core self (which other animals have) to an autobiographical identity through intuition, mirror, and canonical neurons, using inner simulations of the Other to form the conscious Self. As with infants today in the mirror stage, and all of us later in life, especially in theatrical situations, the character of Self in our prehistoric relatives developed through interactions with the Other: from "the specular *I* . . . into the social *I*."[38] This involves using reflective images from the Other's apparent perceptions to form simulations of the Other's simulation of me, and putting those into the developing plot of autobiographical memories, fantasies, and dreams. The social Other for Ice Age humans included few contacts with other persons—just a small tribal group as extended family, occasional meetings with other groups, and no mass-media images. But the natural environment did involve many fellow animals. Some were impressively large creatures, which became the dominant images in the caves. Today, like our prehistoric ancestors, we have remnant animal drives within our nervous system, as a "fragmented body" moving in contradictory ways behind the mask of Self and its body image (or gestalt). Lacan sees this exemplified in the human infant's normally premature birth,[39] with an uncoordinated, libidinal body to the age of eighteen months, finding a jubilant yet illusory wholeness in its mirror image (which fixes and reverses it) and in its multisensory interactions with the (m)Other. The protoself, monitoring interior body states, and the core self, interacting physically with the world, are not fully unified in their mappings; their dispositions are divergent as well as convergent (in Damasio's terms).

Theatrical spaces and images in prehistoric caves show particular instances of mirror-stage interactions between early humans and their minds' projections onto the rock walls, probably involving (1) their basic animal drives, (2) remembered animal forms from their environment, and (3) animal characters or fluid animal-human hybrids from their inner brain theatres, including mythic plots as well as handprints and other signs that we can no longer read. We cannot know what the bison- or lion-headed human in Chauvet meant to its creators, or the full plot of the bison charging the stick-man in Villars. But we can receive communications in imaginary, if not symbolic, ways from the reality of mirror-stage performances in cave theatres, related to our own in many other media. The animal or animal-human Other depicted on the cave wall or envisioned through the rock membrane became a way for early humans to develop an image of Self as part of the natural world and yet evolve beyond it, as we are continuing to do. But our ancestors tens of thousands of years ago were just starting to develop the illusions and realities of human ego power over animals and nature, which we magnify with our big brains, artwork, and technology today. So they made far fewer images of the human form.

Even now, though, children often dream of wild animals, while having little or no contact with them in reality. Dream researcher Antii Revonsuo theorizes that our dreams, like those of other mammals, may have evolved as "threat rehearsals" for survival in real life and that we carry in our brain structures the prehistoric images that haunted our ancestors for thousands of years, helping them survive and produce us.[40] As we mature in our modern world, we absorb images from its threats and goals to rehearse in our dreams, masking our ancestors' interactions with "wild" animals as natural dangers, food sources, and spirit guides—though they may appear again, even in domestic forms, as urban invaders, tame livestock, or lovable pets. In this sense, too, we experience some of the meaningful features in prehistoric cave theatres through the darkness of our dreams.

The many overlapping images in cave paintings and etchings may show the prehistoric threats of humans to one another, as well as the depths of each person's visionary perceptions through the rock wall. Like graffiti artists today, cave performers might have competed to present their tribal or personal totem, overwriting those of others. And yet the mixture of animal outlines also suggests the source of such ego and group aggression in each of us: the fragmented body behind the Self, which finds an illusory wholeness in the mirror or theatrical image, as display and gaze of the Other. The Self is thus a fragile character, alienated by the Other's misrecognitions and social demands. This produces, even in the mirror-stage infant, a defensive "armor" of Self, masking its own fragility and inherent paranoia, which sometimes results in aggression toward others, especially those figured as evil.[41]

The cave theatres of Spain and France, along with Herzog's film of the Chauvet Cave, show particular mappings of the "extended minds"[42] of our prehistoric ancestors related to the mirror stage that we each pass through as infants, the media screens where we find ideal egos of Self and ego ideals of the Other watching throughout our lives, and the mappings that our inner brain theatres perform. With their theatrical figures and spaces, prehistoric caves reflect how the brains of our ancestors—like ours today—filtered numerous multisensory perceptions of reality to interpret their significance through memories, goals, and fantasies, using primal (animal drive) mappings and higher-order dispositions from the unconscious mind to the conscious Self and awareness of the Other. Such mirror mappings inside our heads, expressed in current theatrical media, can be illuminated by exploring prehistoric caves and considering what their images might have meant in the past, like and unlike today.

Subsequent religious traditions repressed the animist insights of prehistoric cave performers and "pagan" shamans with sky gods and monotheisms. On the medieval European stage, for example, a monstrous cave mouth represented Hell.[43] If we dig back through the layers of such cultural ideals, and through the ancient Greek "birth" of theatre, to imagine cave theatricality in prehistory, then a primal Thespis might be glimpsed in the many handprints, abstract shapes, animal forms, and animal-human hybrid figures of specific chambers and their rock-wall scenery. Such artwork by Thespian shamans may remind us that in becoming human and machine, in the past and future stages of evolution, we are still animals—and sometimes "wild" beyond our dreams. The prehistoric performers' paintings and engravings reflect how we use each other, even today, as animals and media figures to map the fragments of Self into transcendent yet illusory characters, which have real effects on our continuing biological and cultural evolution.

Notes

1. See also Mark Pizzato, *Inner Theatres of Good and Evil: The Mind's Staging of Gods, Angels and Devils* (Jefferson, NC: McFarland, 2011), for details on another dozen caves that I visited in 2009.

2. Yann-Pierre Montelle, *Palaeoperformance* (London: Seagull, 2009); Yann-Pierre Montelle, "Paleoperformance: Investigating the Human Use of Caves in the Upper Paleolithic," in *New Perspectives on Prehistoric Art*, ed. Günter Berghaus (Westport, CT: Praeger, 2004), 131–52; "Mimicry, Deception, Mimesis," *Rock Art Research* 23, no. 1 (2006): 23–24.

3. Jean Clottes and David Lewis-Williams, *The Shamans of Prehistory: Trance and Magic in the Painted Caves*, trans. Sophie Hawkes (New York: Abrams, 1998). For a critique of such a "magico-religious" theory, see zoologist R. Dale Guthrie, *The Nature of Paleolithic Art* (Chicago: University of Chicago Press, 2005), 8–9, 36, 413, 427. In support of the theory, with a focus on Chauvet, see David S. Whitley, *Cave Paintings and the Human Spirit* (New York: Prometheus, 2009). See also Jean Clottes, *Cave Art* (London: Phaidon, 2008), for its photos and timeline.

4. On the relation of cave surfaces to prehistoric paintings, see Masaru Ogawa, "Integration in Franco-Cantabrian Parietal Art," in *Aesthetics and Rock Art*, ed. Thomas Heyd and John Clegg (Hampshire, UK: Ashgate, 2005), 117–30.

5. Montelle, "Paleoperformance," 134–36.

6. For photos of the Chauvet Cave, see Jean Clottes, *Chauvet Cave* (Salt Lake

City: University of Utah Press, 2003); and Gregory Curtis, *The Cave Painters* (New York: Knopf, 2006).

7. Cf. David Lewis-Williams, "Of People and Pictures," in *Becoming Human*, ed. Colin Renfrew and Iain Morley (Cambridge: Cambridge University Press, 2009), 146, 150.

8. Clottes, *Chauvet Cave*, 99.

9. David Lewis-Williams, *The Mind in the Cave* (London: Thames and Hudson, 2002), 258.

10. Red and black paint were also combined in an unusual way for purple shading at Tito Bustillo. And there is a figure that may be a whale. For those traveling to the cave, which is across the river Sella from Ribadesella, there is a nice interpretive center, and tickets may be booked in advance by phone. It is also within a sixty- to ninety-minute drive of the two other Asturian caves described in this essay, El Pindal and El Buxu, but they are more difficult to reach, requiring travel on winding, narrow mountain roads sometimes shared by grazing cattle, and long walks to the caves from small parking areas. Reservations should be made, especially at the more remote caves, since guides are not always present. At all three, tours are free on Wednesdays and cost just three euros on other days. Entrance to caves in France usually costs six euros for adults.

11. See Antonio Beltrán, ed., *The Cave of Altamira* (New York: Harry N. Abrams, 1999).

12. Cf. Lewis-Williams, *The Mind in the Cave*, 36–37. He also details other chambers of the Altamira Cave.

13. See Pizzato, *Inner Theatres*, 39.

14. Cf. Lewis-Williams, *The Mind in the Cave*, 204.

15. It is difficult, yet possible, to visit all five Cantabrian caves described in this essay in just one day, with sixty to ninety minutes of travel time needed between them, except for the adjacent caves, El Castillo and Las Monedas. Those two have a large parking lot and interpretive center, but the other caves are on narrow mountain roads near small villages (though El Pendo is also near the large city of Santander). Tour reservations may be booked online.

16. Jacques Lacan, *Écrits*, trans. Bruce Fink (New York: Norton, 2006), 78.

17. Cf. Montelle, *Palaeoperformance*, 85–86, on his experience of "fragmentation" in the Gargas Cave.

18. Jacques Lacan, *The Four Fundamental Concepts of Psycho-Analysis*, trans. Alan Sheridan (New York: Norton, 1981), 82, 86–89.

19. Cf. Georges Bataille, *Lascaux* (Switzerland: Skira, 1955), 27–36.

20. Merlin Donald, *A Mind So Rare: The Evolution of Human Consciousness* (New York: Norton, 2001), 120, 255, 260–74; cf. Colin Renfrew, "Situating the Creative Explosion," in *Becoming Human*, ed. Colin Renfrew and Iain Morley (Cambridge: Cambridge University Press, 2009), 74–92, who finds evidence of "artistic patterning" in pierced shells, which were probably used as beads seventy thousand years ago in southern Africa. Those may also show the emergence of Self awareness in a new way.

21. See Stephen Mithen, *The Prehistory of the Mind* (London: Thames and

Hudson, 1996), 140–42, 163–65, 208. Lewis-Williams relates Mithen's theory to his own about cave art in *The Mind in the Cave*, 107–11.

22. Julia Kristeva, *Revolution in Poetic Language* (New York: Columbia University Press, 1984), 28.

23. Stephen Mithen, "The Evolution of Imagination: An Archaeological Perspective," *Sub-Stance* 94/95 (2001): 48–50.

24. Unlike Merveilles, the Gargas Cave (with a small museum) is on a winding mountain road and difficult to reach ; it is west of Saint-Gaudens, in the area of Aventignan.

25. Curtis, *The Cave Painters,* 196–97.

26. Lewis-Williams, *The Mind in the Cave*, 216–20.

27. Frans de Waal, *Our Inner Ape* (New York: Penguin, 2005), 240–41.

28. See Bernard Baars, *In the Theater of Consciousness* (Oxford: Oxford University Press, 1997). The meaning of brain theatre here, as in Baars, is different from the much-debated "Cartesian theatre," which involves a dualist sense of mind controlling brain, of reason over matter.

29. The Villars Cave is about an hour's drive north of Périgueux, near the tiny village of Le Cluzeau.

30. Curtis, in *The Cave Painters*, sees it as a provocation (118). Comparing this with another bison-and-man scene in Lascaux, he calls it a "universal myth."

31. There are about seventy-five anthropomorphic figures in all of prehistoric cave art, a very small percentage of the total discovered. Lewis-Williams, in *The Mind in the Cave*, makes comparisons with southern African (San) and Native American rock art, which involve many human figures: "Some societies focus on animals as sources of power or as helpers, while others emphasize anthropomorphic depictions of shamans and spirits" (277).

32. Damasio agrees with the Freudian theory of the unconscious in relation to a conscious self as "an internal and imperfectly constructed informer rather than an external, reliable observer." Antonio Damasio, *Self Comes to Mind: Constructing the Conscious Brain* (New York: Pantheon, 2010), 177. He also calls the self a "virtual element: an imagined *protagonist* of our mental events" (166). I use the term "Self" with a capital S (though Damasio does not) to designate this sense of a reflective, illusory ego in human consciousness. I also use "Other" with a capital O in the Lacanian sense of a social network with ideals of Self (ideal egos), and of others or gods (ego ideals) watching the Self. For more on these ghosts of Self and Other, see Mark Pizzato, *Ghosts of Theatre and Cinema in the Brain* (New York: Palgrave, 2006). See also Todd E. Feinberg, *Altered Egos: How the Brain Creates the Self* (Oxford: Oxford University Press, 2011), and V. S. Ramachandran, *The Tell-Tale Brain* (New York: Norton, 2011), 250–88.

33. See the essays by David F. Bjorklund and Katherine Kipp, by Richard Byrne, and by Michael C. Corballis in *The Evolution of Intelligence*, ed. Robert J. Sternberg and James C. Kaufman (Mahwah, NJ: Lawrence Erlbaum, 2002). See also Dorothy L. Cheney and Robert M. Seyfarth, *Baboon Metaphysics: The Evolution of a Social Mind* (Chicago: University of Chicago Press, 2007).

34. See Marco Iacoboni, *Mirroring People* (New York: Farrar, 2008). See also

Pierre Jacob and Marc Jeannerod, *Ways of Seeing* (Oxford: Oxford University Press, 2003), 230–34; and Ramachandran, *Tell-Tale Brain*, 117–52.

35. See Vittorio Gallese and Alvin Goldman, "Mirror Neurons and the Simulation Theory of Mind-Reading," *Trends in Cognitive Neuroscience* 2, no. 12 (1998): 493–502; and Sandra Blakeslee and Matthew Blakeslee, *The Body Has a Mind of Its Own* (New York: Random House, 2007).

36. See Elaine Hatfield, John T. Cacioppo, and Richard L. Rapson, *Emotional Contagion* (Cambridge: Cambridge University Press, 1994); and Ellen S. Sullins, "Emotional Contagion Revisited," *Personality and Social Psychology Bulletin* 17, no. 2 (1991): 166–74.

37. Giacomo Rizzolatti and Corrado Sinigaglia, *Mirrors in the Brain: How Our Minds Share Our Actions, Emotions, and Experience* (Oxford: Oxford University Press, 2008), 151.

38. Lacan, *Écrits*, 79.

39. In comparison with other apes, humans are born nine to fifteen months early, due to our large brain and limits to the size of a two-legged mother's birth canal.

40. Antti Revonsuo, "The Reinterpretation of Dreams: An Evolutionary Hypothesis of the Function of Dreaming," in *Sleeping and Dreaming*, ed. Edward F. Pace-Schott, Mark Solms, Mark Blagrove, and Stevan Harnad (Cambridge: Cambridge University Press, 2003), 85–111.

41. Lacan, *Écrits*, 78–79.

42. See Richard Menary, ed., *The Extended Mind* (Cambridge: MIT Press, 2010).

43. Even today, *Hölle* is the word for both "cave" and "Hell" in German. Yet Our Lady of Lourdes, site of a nineteenth-century vision by a girl in a grotto in the Pyrenees near Gargas, is still valued by many Catholics as a miracle-working image and site.

Excerpts from "The Book of

My Awkward Perspective"

William Doan

Bill Doan, president of the Association for Theatre in Higher Education (ATHE) and professor of theatre at Penn State, attended Theatre Symposium as a conference respondent and friend of SETC. His work combines poetry, religion, and theatre; we were honored by his presence and by his two-part performance (split between the beginning and end of the conference). Several of the poems embedded in the work were first published as orantes linguis, *(Corrupt Press, November 2011). While, regrettably, space limitations will not allow the text of the entire performance and response to be printed here, we are pleased to include a few excerpts.*

We are gathered here by connections, intersections, appropriations, and clashes between ritual, religion, and theatre.

- Historical uses of theatre by religious establishments
- Religious opposition to theatre
- Ah—but what about theatrical opposition to religion?
- Ritual in performance studies
- Performance in ritual studies
- Worship in or as performance
- Performance in or as worship
- Clashes, practices, uses, understandings
AND . . .
- Et cetera

Clearly Bert, out of concern for something to meet the weighty expectations of "et cetera," saw a golden opportunity to include my work. After seven years of collaboration on two books with a Hebrew Bible scholar (Terry Giles), I did what any theatre artist would do . . . ignoring Umberto Eco's rules for walking through a fictional woods, I over-identified with the characters of that ancient Hebrew world where prayer was an act of the body and the chaos of adapting to obeying one God left people tangled and confused. So, as someone who hails from the land of the tangled and confused, I offer you . . .

Patriarchy, hierarchy,
In the midst of the Our Father,
the *pater noster*, Matthew's debts, Luke's trespasses,
sins, transgressions, and a two source hypothesis, *I
Heard*, my child, speak the speech I pray you as I
pronounced it to you. Pragmatically, with your whole body,
for by your wounds and scars shall you be known.

Our Father Who Art in Heaven
Hail Mary Full of Grace
Oh My God I am Heartily Sorry
Again.
Our Father Who Art in Heaven
Hail Mary Full of Grace
Oh My God I am Heartily Sorry
Again.
. . . .
In the absence of the Father and of the Son and of the Holy Spirit.
Stupid little bastard who believes in heaven
hallowed be the lawnmower.
Thy blades they come, thy will be done,
with any stray sticks and rocks on the ground.
And give me this day my daily lesson
as I forgive those sticks and stones that trespass against me.
And lead me not to another beating,
but deliver me from waiting.
. . . .
Constructing narratives, deconstructing narratives,
embodying, performing, and explicating.
We inhabited new spaces, metaphorical and
other. Neuronal pathways serving perhaps
as liminal gestures taking us, once again,
through the looking glass, past what it might
be reflecting back, and on to a detour journey -

A cognitive/performative/embodied/liturgical/
communitas of the gut . . .

That which keeps us tangled up with our
rituals, ceremonies, and entertainments,
carrying the histories of worshippers and non
scattered across all of human time and space.
Histories also tangled up by the reproductive
mingling of those histories with the multi-hyphened
identities of all gathered here.

We witnessed wonderful moments on Tom
Driver's "playground of the maybe," looking over
our shoulders at maybe not, but ending, for me,
with the "blessed assurance of perhaps."[1]

Theatrical presentation, wrote Bernard Beckerman,
is rooted in the tradition of the gift-a thing given
out of love and respect, received by another.
This Symposium was a gift for me. Thank you.

Notes

1. Quotes are taken from Dr. Tom Driver's keynote address at the SETC Theatre Symposium, April 20, 2012, University of North Carolina–Wilmington.

Contributors

Cohen Ambrose is an MA in theatre studies and an MFA directing candidate at the University of Montana, Missoula. A native of Montana, Cohen has lived and worked in Montana, Washington State, New York City, and Prague, Czech Republic. His research interests include cognitive studies in performance, Brecht, theatre pedagogy, physical performance methodologies, and European cultural and intellectual history. Cohen writes, directs, teaches, performs, and spends a lot of time in the mountains.

David Callaghan has presented numerous papers on 1960s performance, training for actors and directors, and musical theatre development at ATHE and Theatre Symposium conferences. He has published work about the Living Theatre and 1960s performance in *American Theatre, Theatre Journal, Works and Days, Theatre Symposium,* and *The Journal of Dramatic Theory and Criticism*. He worked with the Living Theatre as the assistant director on its premiere of *Rules of Civility . . .* in 1991. He received his MFA in directing from Western Illinois University and a PhD in theatre from the CUNY Graduate Center in Manhattan. David is professor and chair of theatre at the University of Montevallo near Birmingham, Alabama.

Gregory S. Carr is a graduate of the MFA Acting Program of the University of Illinois Urbana–Champaign. He has directed numerous shows (including *God's Trombones* in 2012) and presented on playwright August Wilson (as well as directing plays by Wilson). Gregory's paper "Three Fridays in August: Black Male Bonding in *Fences*" was selected by the

National Association of African American Studies (NAAAS) and presented at their national conference in February 2009. Gregory is also a produced playwright whose plays include *Johnnie Taylor Is Gone*, *A Colored Funeral*, and *Stormy Monday*, the latter was given a staged reading at the National Black Theatre Festival in Winston-Salem, North Carolina. Gregory is an instructor of speech and theatre at Harris-Stowe State University in Saint Louis, Missouri.

Matt DiCintio received his MFA in theatre pedagogy at Virginia Commonwealth University and is pursuing his PhD at Tufts University. Publications include contributions to *American Theatre Magazine*, the *Columbia Encyclopedia of Modern Drama*, and the *Tennessee Williams Annual Review*. Matt's research interests include new play development and queer theatre.

William Doan is a professor of theatre at Penn State University. He currently serves as president of the Association for Theatre in Higher Education (ATHE). In addition to his numerous scholarly publications and creative performances, he is the coauthor with Terry Giles of *Prophets, Performance and Power* (2005) and *Twice Used Songs: Performance Criticism of the Songs of Ancient Israel* (2008).

Tom F. Driver is the Paul J. Tillich Professor of Theology and Culture Emeritus at Union Theological Seminary in New York, where he taught for many years. He is the author of *Liberating Rites: Understanding the Transformative Power of Ritual*, *Romantic Quest and Modern Query: A History of the Modern Theatre*, and numerous other works. He has been the drama critic for *The Christian Century*, *The Reporter*, radio station WBAI-FM in New York, and other venues. He is widely published in the fields of ritual, religion, theatre, and human rights concerns. Much of his scholarly and humanitarian work has been focused on Haiti, where he has traveled frequently.

Steve Earnest is associate professor of theatre at Coastal Carolina University in Myrtle Beach, South Carolina. A member of the Screen Actors Guild and Actor's Equity, he has worked professionally with numerous professional theatre companies in the United States as well as a growing number of film projects in the southeast. He has been published in *Theatre Journal*, *Backstage West*, *Ecumenica*, *The Journal of Beckett Studies*, *Theatre Symposium*, *New Theatre Quarterly*, and *Theatre Studies*, among others. In 1999 he published a book, *The State Acting Academy of East*

Berlin, and is currently working on a book about the theatre system of Iceland.

Jennifer Flaherty received her PhD in comparative literature from the University of North Carolina–Chapel Hill. Her work on Shakespeare and Shakespearean adaptation has been published in the journal *Topic*, *The Columbia Encyclopedia of Modern Drama*, and the recent book *The Horse as Cultural Icon*. She is an assistant professor of Shakespeare at Georgia College and State University.

Charles A. Gillespie graduated summa cum laude from the Villanova University Honors Program with a BA in humanities. Charlie is currently an MA candidate in religion at Yale Divinity School and the Yale Institute of Sacred Music, concentrating his studies on theology and the arts.

Thomas King holds a PhD in theatre from Indiana University. He is an emeritus professor of theatre at James Madison University and was Fulbright senior lecturer in American studies at Hacettepe University in Ankara, Turkey. In 1996 he attended an NEH seminar titled "Islamic History and Cultures," which inspired him to include discussions of Muslim theatre in his teaching and to present scholarly work on Muslim theatre and performance at ATHE and Performance Studies International in an ongoing effort to make students and others aware of Muslim performance.

Justin Kosec is a Master of Divinity candidate at Yale Divinity School. He served as a Marquand Chapel minister at YDS for the 2011–2012 school year. He is an endorsed candidate for ordination in the Minneapolis Area Synod of the Evangelical Lutheran Church of America.

Mark Pizzato, MFA, PhD, is professor of theatre at the University of North Carolina–Charlotte, where he teaches playwriting, screenwriting, theatre history, dramaturgy, performance theory, and other topics in theatre and film. His writings include *Inner Theatres of Good and Evil: The Mind's Staging of Gods, Angels and Devils* (McFarland 2011), *Ghosts of Theatre and Cinema in the Brain* (Palgrave 2006), and *Theatres of Human Sacrifice: From Ancient Ritual to Screen Violence* (SUNY 2005). He has also published several plays. Short films produced from his screenplays have won New York Film Festival and Minnesota Community Television awards. He has served on the editorial boards of *Ecumenica* since 2004 and the *Journal of Religion and Theatre* since 2008.

Kate Stratton graduated from the University of North Carolina–Chapel Hill with a dual bachelor's in music and dramatic art. She recently completed her Master of Divinity degree at Yale Divinity School, where she is remaining to develop a Master of Sacred Theology thesis project in drama and liturgy.